GROWING IN CHRISTIAN FAITH

Growing in Christian Faith

A Book of Daily Readings

WILLIAM BARCLAY

Westminster John Knox Press
Louisville, Kentucky

© 2000 Westminster John Knox Press
Materials reproduced from the Daily Study Bible, revised edition,
are copyright © 1975, 1976 William Barclay.

Book design by Sharon Adams
Cover design by Jennifer Cox

First edition
Published by Westminster John Knox Press
Louisville, Kentucky

This book is printed on acid-free paper that meets
the American National Standards Institute Z39.48 standard. ∞

PRINTED IN THE UNITED STATES OF AMERICA
00 01 02 03 04 05 06 07 08 09—10 9 8 7 6 5 4 3 2 1

Library of Congress Cataloging-in-Publication Data

Barclay, William, 1907–1978.
    Growing in Christian faith : a book of daily readings / William Barclay. — 1st ed.
        p. cm.
    ISBN 0-664-22227-7 (alk. paper)
    1. Christian life—Meditations. 2. Devotional calendars. I. Title.

 BV4501.2 .B38246 2000
 242'.2—dc21   99-048059

Contents

Introduction

"Do not be conformed to this world, but be transformed by the renewing of your minds, so that you may discern what is the will of God—what is good and acceptable and perfect."

If all of the strength, beauty and wisdom of the New Testament could be summed up in just a few words, that phrase might be "God is love." The life-giving message of the scriptures that "the truth shall set you free" breaks the seemingly endless search by individuals to find meaning and salvation through their own self-determination. Recognizing God's love for us is the truth that sets us free.

But the depth and richness of the New Testament goes beyond this simple phrase. The real accounts of God's people also adorn its pages. Their struggles and stories give witness to a faith that nurtures growth in Christian discipleship.

William Barclay, in his Daily Study Bible, disclosed the treasure of scripture through his ability to provide accurate and picturesque explanations. He brought to life Jesus' feelings, teachings and relationships in ways that carry the reader back in time to hear the words as if Jesus himself were speaking. Barclay's gift for writing enables those of every stage and age to comprehend and apply God's message to their lives.

In this little book are daily devotions drawn from the Daily Study Bible for those seeking transformation through the renewing of their minds. The topics were chosen because of their clear and dramatic presentation of God's intent and will for our lives—for that which is good and acceptable and perfect. The temptation in our world today is to "water down" the sacrifices and demands of Christian discipleship, and to conform to an easier, less rigorous philosophy. This collection of a month's worth of meditations challenges the reader otherwise.

The insights of William Barclay that are collected in *Growing in Christian Faith* have three basic themes. First, God cares for the world like a parent does for a child. Second, we should treat others not as the law allows, but as love demands. Third, salvation is offered to us at great cost as a gift from God, and should not be accepted cavalierly.

It is my hope that after reading the selected passages and accompanying commentary, the reader will have a greater appreciation for the Bible's life-giving words and power to change attitudes. However we come to scripture, early or late, willingly or at first reluctantly, God's truth can set us free. May we claim that truth openly, confidently and obediently.

Ferd Wagner

DAY ONE

The Place of Material Possessions

Matthew 6:24

No man can be a slave to two owners; for either he will hate the one and love the other, or he will cleave to the one and despise the other. You cannot be a slave to God and to material things.

This saying of Jesus' is bound to turn our thoughts to the place which material possessions should have in life. At the basis of Jesus' teaching about possessions there are three great principles.

(i) In the last analysis *all things belong to God.* Scripture makes that abundantly clear. "The earth is the Lord's and the fullness thereof; the world and those who dwell therein" (*Psalm* 24:1). "For every beast of the forest is mine, the cattle on a thousand hills. . . . If I were hungry I would not tell you, for the world and all that is in it is mine" (*Psalm* 50:10,12).

In Jesus' teaching it is the master who gives his servants the talents (*Matthew* 25:15) and the owner who gives the husbandman the vineyard (*Matthew* 21:33). This principle has far-reaching consequences. Men can buy and sell things; men can to some extent alter and rearrange things; but man cannot create things. The ultimate ownership of all things belongs to God. There is nothing in this world of which a man can say, "This is mine." Of all things he can only say, "This belongs to God, and God has given me the use of it."

Therefore this basic principle of life emerges. There is nothing in this world of which any man can say, "This is mine, and I will therefore do what I like with it." Of everything he *must* say, "This is God's and I must use it as its owner would have it to be used." There is a story of a city child who was taken for a day in the country. For the first time in her life she saw a drift of bluebells. She turned to her teacher and said, "Do you think God would mind if I picked one of his flowers?" That is the correct attitude to life and all things in the world.

(ii) The second basic principle is that *people are always more important than things.* If possessions have to be acquired, if money has to be amassed, if wealth has to be accumulated at the expense of treating people as things, then all such riches are wrong. Whenever and wherever that principle is forgotten, or neglected, or defied, far-reaching disaster is certain to follow.

In this country we are to this day suffering in the world of industrial relationships from the fact that in the days of the industrial revolution people were treated as things. Sir Arthur Bryant in *English Saga* tells of some of the things which happened in those days. Children of seven and eight years of age—there is actually a case of a child of three—were employed in the mines. Some of them dragged trucks along galleries on all fours; some of them pumped out water standing knee-deep in the water for twelve hours a day; some of them, called trappers, opened and shut the ventilating doors of the shafts, and were shut into little ventilating chambers for as much as sixteen hours a day. In 1815 children were working in the mills from 5 A.M. to 8 P.M. without even a Saturday half-holiday, and with half an hour off for breakfast and half an hour off for dinner. In 1833 there were eighty-four thousand children under fourteen in the factories. There is actually a case recorded in which the children whose labor was no longer required were taken to a common and turned adrift. The owners objected to the expression "turned adrift." They said that the children had been set at liberty. They agreed that the children might find things hard. "They would have to beg their way or something of that sort." In 1842 the weavers of Burnley were being paid 7 1/2 d. a day, and the miners of Staffordshire 2s. 6d. a day. There were those who saw the criminal folly of all this. Carlyle thundered, "If the cotton industry is founded on the bodies of rickety children, it must go; if the devil gets in your cotton-mill, shut the mill." It was pleaded that cheap labor was necessary to keep costs down. Coleridge answered, "You talk about making this article cheaper by reducing its price in the market from 8d. to 6d. But suppose in so doing you have rendered your country weaker against a foreign foe; suppose you have demoralized thousands of your fellow-countrymen, and have sown discontent between one class of society and another, your article is tolerably dear, I take it, after all."

It is perfectly true that things are very different nowadays. But there is such a thing as racial memory. Deep in the unconscious memory of people the impression of these bad days is indelibly impressed. Whenever people are treated as things, as machines, as instruments for producing so much labor and for enriching those who employ them, then as certainly as the night follows the day disaster follows. A nation forgets at its peril the principle that people are always more important than things.

(iii) The third principle is that *wealth is always a subordinate good.* The Bible does not say that "Money is the root of all evil"; it says that "*The love of money* is the root of all evils" (*1 Timothy* 6:10). It is quite possible to find in material things what someone has called "a rival salvation." A man may think that, because he is wealthy, he can buy anything, that he can buy his way out of any situation. Wealth can become his measuring-rod; wealth can become his one desire; wealth can become the one weapon with which he faces life. If a man desires material things for an honorable independence, to help his family and to do something for his fellow-men, that is good; but if he desires it simply to heap pleasure upon pleasure, and to add luxury, if wealth has become the thing he lives for and lives by, then wealth has ceased to be a subordinate good, and has usurped the place in life which only God should occupy.

One thing emerges from all this—the possession of wealth, money, material things is not a sin, but it is a grave *responsibility.* If a man owns many material things it is not so much a matter for congratulation as it is a matter for prayer, that he may use them as God would have him to do.

DAY TWO

A Convincing Story

Acts 11:11–18

"And, look you, thereupon, three men, who had been sent to me from Caesarea, stood at the house where we were. The Spirit told me to go with them

*and to make no distinctions. These six brethren also came with me and
we came to the man's house. He told us how in the house he had seen the
angel standing and saying, 'Send to Joppa and send for Simon, who is also
called Peter, who will speak words to you by which you and all your house
will be saved.' As I was beginning to speak, the Holy Spirit fell upon them,
just as in the beginning he did upon you. And I remembered the Lord's
word and how he said, 'John baptized you with water but you will be
baptized with the Holy Spirit.' If God gave the same gift to them as to us
who have believed in the Lord Jesus Christ, who was I to be able to hin-
der God?" When they heard this they had no protests to make and they
glorified God saying, "So God has given life-giving repentance to the Gentiles too."*

The fault for which Peter was initially on trial was that he had eaten
with Gentiles (verse 3). By so doing Peter had outraged the ancestral
Law and traditions of his people. Peter's defense was not an argument;
it was a statement of the facts. Whatever his critics might say the Holy
Spirit had come upon these Gentiles in the most notable way. In verse
12 there is a significant sidelight. Peter says that he took six brethren
with him. Together with himself that made seven persons present. In
Egyptian law, which the Jews would know well, seven witnesses were
necessary completely to prove a case. In Roman law, which they
would also know well, seven seals were necessary to authenticate a really important document. So Peter is in effect saying, "I am not arguing with you. I am telling you the facts and of these facts there are
seven witnesses. The case is proved."

The proof of Christianity always lies in facts. It is doubtful if anyone has ever been argued into Christianity by verbal proofs and logical demonstrations. The proof of Christianity is that it works, that
it does change men, that it does make bad men good, that it does
bring to men the Spirit of God. It is when a man's deeds give the lie
to his words that the gravest discredit is brought on Christianity; it
is when a man's words are guaranteed by his deeds that the world is
presented with an argument for Christianity which will brook no
denial.

DAY THREE

Our Daily Bread

Matthew 6:11

Give us to-day bread for the coming day.

One would have thought that this is the one petition of the Lord's Prayer about the meaning of which there could have been no possible doubt. It seems on the face of it to be the simplest and the most direct of them all. But it is the fact that many interpreters have offered many interpretations of it. Before we think of its simple and obvious meaning, let us look at some of the other explanations which have been offered.

(i) The bread has been identified with the bread of the Lord's Supper. From the very beginning the Lord's Prayer has been closely connected with the Lord's Table. In the very first orders of service which we possess it is always laid down that the Lord's Prayer should be prayed at the Lord's Table, and some have taken this petition as a prayer to be granted the daily privilege of sitting at the Table of our Lord, and of eating the spiritual food which a man receives there.

(ii) The bread has been identified with the spiritual food of the word of God. We sometimes sing the hymn:

Break thou the bread of life,
Dear Lord, to me,
As thou didst break the loaves
Beside the sea.
Beyond the sacred page
I seek thee, Lord,
My Spirit pants for thee,
O living word.

So this petition has been taken to be a prayer for the true teaching, the true doctrine, the essential truth, which are in the scriptures and the word of God, and which are indeed food for a man's heart and soul.

(iii) The bread has been taken to stand for Jesus himself. Jesus called himself *the bread of life* (*John* 6:33–35), and this has been taken to be a prayer that daily we may be fed on him who is the living bread. It was in that way that Matthew Arnold used the phrase, when he wrote his poem about the saint of God he met in the east end of London one suffocating day:

> 'Twas August, and the fierce sun overhead
> Smote on the squalid streets of Bethnal Green,
> And the pale weaver, through his windows seen,
> In Spitalfields, look'd thrice dispirited.
>
> I met a preacher there I knew and said:
> "Ill and o'er worked, how fare you in this scene?"
> "Bravely!" said he, "for I of late have been
> Much cheer'd with thoughts of Christ, the living bread."

(iv) The bread has been taken to be the bread of the heavenly kingdom. Luke tells how one of the bystanders said to Jesus, "Blessed is he who shall eat bread in the Kingdom of God" (*Luke* 14:15). The Jews had a strange yet vivid idea. They held that when the Messiah came, and when the golden age dawned, there would be what they called the Messianic banquet, at which the chosen ones of God would sit down. The slain bodies of the monsters Behemoth and Leviathan would provide the meat and the fish courses of the banquet. It would be a kind of reception feast given by God to his own people. So, then, this has been taken to be a petition for a place at the final Messianic banquet of the people of God.

Although we need not agree that any one of these explanations is the main meaning of this petition, we need not reject any of them as false. They all have their own truth and their own relevance.

The difficulty of interpreting this petition was increased by the fact that there was very considerable doubt as to the meaning of the word *epiousios,* which is the word which the Revised Standard Version translates *daily.* The extraordinary fact was that, until a short time ago, there was no other known occurrence of this word in the whole of Greek literature. It was therefore not possible to be sure what it precisely meant. But not very long ago a papyrus fragment turned up with this word on it; and the papyrus fragment was actually a woman's shopping list! And against an item on it was the word *epiousios.* It was a note to remind her to buy supplies of a certain food for the coming day. So very simply what this petition means is: "Give me the things we need to eat for this coming day. Help me to get the things I've got on my shopping list when I go out this morning. Give me the things we need to eat when the children come in from school, and the men folk come in from work. Grant that the table be not bare when we sit down together to-day." This is a simple prayer that God will supply us with the things we need for the coming day.

When we see that this is a simple petition for the needs of the everyday, certain tremendous truths emerge from it.

(v) It tells us that God cares for our bodies. Jesus showed us that; he spent so much time healing men's diseases and satisfying their physical hunger. He was anxious when he thought that the crowds who had followed him out into the lonely places had a long road home, and no food to eat before they set out upon it. We do well to remember that God is interested in our bodies. Any teaching which belittles, and despises, and slanders the body is wrong. We can see what God thinks of our human bodies, even we remember that he himself in Jesus Christ took a human body upon him. It is not simply *soul* salvation, it is *whole* salvation, the salvation of body, mind and spirit, at which Christianity aims.

(vi) This petition teaches us to pray for our *daily* bread, for bread *for the coming day.* It teaches us to live one day at a time, and not to worry and be anxious about the distant and the unknown future. When Jesus taught his disciples to pray this petition, there is little doubt that his mind was going back to the story of the manna in the wilderness (*Exodus* 16:1–21). The children of Israel were starving in the wilderness, and God sent them the manna, the food from heaven; but there was the condition—they must gather only enough for their immediate needs. If they tried to gather too much, and to store it up, it went bad. They had to be satisfied with enough for the day. As one Rabbi put it: "The portion of a day in its day, because he who created the day created sustenance for the day." And as another Rabbi had it: "He who possesses what he can eat to-day, and says, 'What shall I eat to-morrow?' is a man of little faith." This petition tells us to live one day at a time. It forbids the anxious worry which is so characteristic of the life which has not learned to trust God.

(vii) By implication this petition gives God his proper place. It admits that it is from God we receive the food which is necessary to support life. No man has ever created a seed which will grow. The scientist can analyze a seed into its constituent elements, but no synthetic seed would ever grow. All living things come from God. Our food, therefore, is the direct gift of God.

(viii) This petition very wisely reminds us how prayer works. If a man prayed this prayer, and then sat back and waited for the bread to fall into his hands, he would certainly starve. It reminds us that prayer and work go hand in hand and that when we pray we must go on to work to make our prayers come true. It is true that the living seed comes from God, but it is equally true that it is man's task to grow and to cultivate that seed. Dick Sheppard used to love a certain story. There was a man who had an allotment; he had with great toil reclaimed a piece of ground, clearing away the stones, eradicating the rank growth of weeds, enriching and feeding the ground, until it produced the loveliest flowers and vegetables. One evening he was showing a pious friend around his allotment. The pious friend said, "It's wonderful what God can do with a bit of ground like this, isn't it?" "Yes," said the man who had put in such toil, "but you should have seen this bit of ground when God had it to himself!" God's bounty and man's toil must combine. Prayer, like faith, without works is dead. When we pray this petition we are recognizing two basic truths—that without God we can do nothing, and that without our effort and co-operation God can do nothing for us.

(ix) We must note that Jesus did not teach us to pray: "Give *me my* daily bread." He taught us to pray: "Give *us our* daily bread." The problem of the world is not that there is not enough to go round; there is enough and to spare. The problem is not the *supply* of life's essentials; it is the *distribution* of them. This prayer teaches us never to be selfish in our prayers. It is a prayer which we can help God to answer by giving to others who are less fortunate than we are. This prayer is not only a prayer that we may *receive* our daily bread; it is also a prayer that we may *share* bread with others.

DAY FOUR

The Mistaken Thinkers

Colossians 1:15–23

He is the image of the invisible God, begotten before all creation, because by him all things were created, in heaven and upon earth, the things which are visible and the things which are invisible, whether thrones or lordships or powers or authorities. All things were created through him and for him. He is before all things, and in him all things cohere. He is the head of the body, that is, of the Church. He is the beginning, the first-born from the dead, that he might be supreme in all things. For in him God in all his fullness was pleased to take up his abode, and through him to reconcile all things to himself, when he had made peace through the blood of his Cross. This was done for all things, whether on the earth or in the heavens. And you, who were once estranged and hostile in your minds, in the midst of evil deeds, he has now reconciled in the body of his flesh, through his death, in order to present you before him consecrated, unblemished, irreproachable, if only you remain grounded and established in the faith, not shifting from the hope of the gospel which you have heard, which has been proclaimed to every creature under heaven, of which I, Paul, have been made a servant.

It is one of the facts of the human mind that a man thinks only as much as he has to. It is not until a man finds his faith opposed and attacked that he really begins to think out its implications. It is not until the Church is confronted with some dangerous heresy that she begins to realize the riches of orthodoxy. It is characteristic of Christianity that it can always produce new riches to meet a new situation.

When Paul wrote *Colossians,* he was not writing in a vacuum. He was writing, as we have already seen in the introduction, to meet a very definite situation. There was a tendency of thought in the early Church called Gnosticism. Its devotees were called *Gnostics,* which more or less means *the intellectual ones.* These men were dissatisfied with what they considered the rude simplicity of Christianity and wished to turn it into a philosophy and to align it with the other philosophies which held the field at that time.

The Gnostics began with the basic assumption that matter was altogether evil and spirit altogether good. They further held that matter was eternal and that it was out of this evil matter that the world was created. The Christian, to use the technical phrase, believes in creation out of nothing; the Gnostic believed in creation out of evil matter.

Now God was spirit and if spirit was altogether good and matter essentially evil, it followed, as the Gnostic saw it, that the true God could not touch matter and, therefore, could not himself be the agent of creation. So the Gnostics believed that God put forth a series of emanations, each a little further away from God until at last there was one so distant from God, that it could handle matter and create the world.

As the emanations went further and further from God, they became more and more ignorant of him. And in the very distant emanations there was not only ignorance of God, but also hostility to him. The Gnostics came to the conclusion that the emanation who created the world was both ignorant of and hostile to the true God; and sometimes they identified that emanation with the God of the Old Testament.

This has certain logical consequences.

(i) As the Gnostics saw it, the creator was not God but someone hostile to him; and the world was not God's world but that of a power hostile to him. That is why Paul insists that God did create the world, and that his agent in creation was no ignorant and hostile emanation but Jesus Christ, his Son (*Colossians* 1:16).

(ii) As the Gnostics saw it, Jesus Christ was by no means unique.

We have seen how they postulated a whole series of emanations between the world and God. They insisted that Jesus was merely one of these emanations. He might stand high in the series; he might even stand highest; but he was only one of many. Paul meets this by insisting that in Jesus Christ all fullness dwells (*Colossians* 1:19); that in him there is the fullness of the godhead in bodily form (*Colossians* 2:9). One of the supreme objects of *Colossians* is to insist that Jesus is utterly unique and that in him there is the whole of God.

(iii) As the Gnostics saw it, this had another consequence with regard to Jesus. If matter was altogether evil, it followed that the body was altogether evil. It followed further that he who was the revelation of God could not have had a real body. He could have been nothing more than a spiritual phantom in bodily form. The Gnostics completely denied the real manhood of Jesus. In their own writings they, for instance, set it down that when Jesus walked, he left no footprints on the ground. That is why Paul uses such startling phraseology in *Colossians*. He speaks of Jesus reconciling man to God *in his body of flesh* (*Colossians* 1:22); he says that the fullness of the godhead dwelt in him *bodily*. In opposition to the Gnostics, Paul insisted on the flesh-and-blood manhood of Jesus.

(iv) The task of man is to find his way to God. As the Gnostics saw it, that way was barred. Between this world and God there was this vast series of emanations. Before the soul could rise to God, it had to get past the barrier of each of these emanations. To pass each barrier, special knowledge and special passwords were needed; it was these passwords and that knowledge that the Gnostics claimed to give. This meant two things.

(a) It meant that salvation was *intellectual knowledge.* To meet that, Paul insists that salvation is not knowledge; it is *redemption* and the *forgiveness of sins.* The Gnostic teachers held that the so-called simple truths of the gospel were not nearly enough. To find its way to God the soul needed far more than that; it needed the elaborate knowledge and the secret passwords which Gnosticism alone could give. So Paul insists that nothing more is needed than the saving truths of the gospel of Jesus Christ.

(b) If salvation depended on this elaborate knowledge, it was clearly not for every man but only for the intellectual. So the Gnostics divided mankind into the spiritual and the earthly; and only the spiritual could be truly saved. Full salvation was beyond the scope of the ordinary man. It is with that in mind that Paul wrote the great verse *Colossians* 1:28. It was his aim to warn *every man* and to teach *every man,* and so to present *every man* mature in Christ Jesus. Against a salvation possible for only a limited intellectual minority, Paul presents a gospel which is for every man, however simple and unlettered or however wise and learned he may be.

DAY FIVE

The Life of Jesus' Chosen People

John 15:11–17

"I have spoken these things to you that my joy might be in you, and that your joy might be complete. This is my commandment, that you love one another, as I have loved you. No one has greater love than this, that a man should lay down his life for his friend. You are my friends, if you do what I command you. I no longer call you slaves, because the slave does not know what his master is doing. I have called you friends because I have made known to you everything that I heard from my Father. You have not chosen me, but I have chosen you, and I have appointed you to go out and to bear fruit, of such a kind that it will remain. I have done so, so that the Father will give you whatever you ask him in my name. These are my orders to you, that you love one another."

The central words of this passage are those in which Jesus says that his disciples have not chosen him, but he has chosen them. It was not we who chose God, but God who, in his grace, approached us with a call and an offer made out of his love.

Out of this passage we can compile a list of things for which we are chosen and to which we are called.

(i) We are chosen for *joy.* However hard the Christian way is, it is, both in the travelling and in the goal, the way of joy. There is always a joy in doing the right thing. The Christian is the man of joy, the laughing cavalier of Christ. A gloomy Christian is a contradiction in terms, and nothing in all religious history has done Christianity more harm than its connection with black clothes and long faces. It is true that the Christian is a sinner, but he is a *redeemed* sinner; and therein lies his joy. How can any man fail to be happy when he walks the ways of life with Jesus?

(ii) We are chosen for *love*. We are sent out into the world to love one another. Sometimes we live as if we were sent into the world to compete with one another, or to dispute with one another, or even to quarrel with one another. But the Christian is to live in such a way that he shows what is meant by loving his fellow men. It is here that Jesus makes another of his great claims. If we ask him: "What right have you to demand that we love one another?" His answer is: "No man can show greater love than to lay down his life for his friends—and I did that." Many a man tells men to love each other, when his whole life is a demonstration that that is the last thing he does himself. Jesus gave men a commandment which he had himself first fulfilled.

(iii) Jesus called us to be *his friends*. He tells his men that he does not call them slaves any more; he calls them friends. Now that is a saying which would be even greater to those who heard it for the first time than it is to us. *Doulos,* the slave, the servant of God, was no title of shame; it was a title of the highest honour. Moses was the *doulos* of God (*Deuteronomy* 34:5); so was Joshua (*Joshua* 24:29); so was David (*Psalm* 89:20). It is a title which Paul counted it an honour to use (*Titus* 1:1); and so did James (*James* 1:1). The greatest men in the past had been proud to be called the *douloi,* the slaves of God. And Jesus says: "I have something greater for you yet, you are no longer *slaves;* you are *friends.*" Christ offers an intimacy with God which not even the greatest men knew before he came into the world.

The idea of being the friend of God has also a background. Abraham was the *friend* of God (*Isaiah* 41:8). In *Wisdom* 7:27 Wisdom is said to make men the friends of God. But this phrase is lit up by a custom which obtained both at the courts of the Roman Emperors and of the eastern kings. At these courts there was a very select group of men called *the friends of the king,* or *the friends of the Emperor.* At all times they had access to the king: they had even the right to come to his bed-chamber at the beginning of the day. He talked to them before he talked to his generals, his rulers and his statesmen. The friends of the king were those who had the closest and the most intimate connection with him.

Jesus called us to be his friends and the friends of God. That is a tremendous offer. It means that no longer do we need to gaze long-ingly at God from afar; we are not like slaves who have no right what-ever to enter into the presence of the master; we are not like a crowd whose only glimpse of the king is in the passing on some state occa-sion. Jesus gave us this intimacy with God, so that he is no longer a distant stranger, but our close friend.

DAY SIX

The Surpassing Glory

2 Corinthians 3:4–11

We can believe this with such confidence because we believe it through Christ and in the sight of God. It is not that in our own resources we are adequate to reckon up the effect of anything that we have done, as it were personally, but our adequacy comes from God, who has made us adequate to be ministers of the new relationship which has come into existence be-tween him and men. This new relationship does not depend on a written document, but on the Spirit. The written document is a deadly thing; the Spirit is a life-giving power. If the ministry which could only produce death, the ministry which depends on written documents, the ministry which was engraved on stone, came into being with such glory that the children of Is-rael could not bear to look for any time at the face of Moses, because of the glory which shone upon his face—and it was a glory that was doomed to fade—surely even more will the ministry of the Spirit be clad in glory. For if the ministry which could not produce anything else but condemnation was a glory, the ministry which produces the right relationship between God and man excels still more in glory. For, indeed, that which was clad with glory no longer enjoys glory because of this—because of the glory that sur-

passes it. If that which was doomed to pass away emerged in glory, much more that which is destined to remain exists in glory.

The new covenant produces between man and God a relationship of a totally different kind.

Wherein does this difference lie?

(i) The old covenant was based on a written document. We can see the story of its initiation in *Exodus* 24:1–8. Moses took the book of the covenant and read it to the people and they agreed to it. On the other hand the new covenant is based on the power of the life-giving Spirit. A written document is always something that is external; whereas the work of the Spirit changes a man's very heart. A man may obey the written code while all the time he wishes to disobey it; but when the Spirit comes into his heart and controls it, not only does he not break the code, he does not even wish to break it, because he is a changed man. A written code can change the law; only the Spirit can change human nature.

(ii) The old covenant was a deadly thing, because it produced a legal relationship between God and man. In effect it said, "If you wish to maintain your relationship with God, you must keep these laws." It thereby set up a situation in which God was essentially judge and man was essentially a criminal, forever in default before the bar of God's judgment.

The old covenant was deadly because it killed certain things. (*a*) It killed *hope*. There was never any hope that any man could keep it, human nature being what it is. It therefore could issue in nothing but frustration. (*b*) It killed *life*. Under it a man could earn nothing but condemnation; and condemnation meant death. (*c*) It killed *strength*. It was perfectly able to tell a man what to do, but it could not help him to do it.

The new covenant was quite different. (*a*) It was a relationship of *love*. It came into being because God so loved the world. (*b*) It was a relationship *between a father and his sons*. Man was no longer the criminal in default, he was the son of God, even if a disobedient son. (*c*) It changed a man's life, not by imposing a new code of laws on him, but *by changing his heart*. (*d*) It therefore not only told a man what to do but gave him the strength to do it. With its commandments *it brought power.*

Paul goes on to contrast the two covenants. The old covenant was born in glory. When Moses came down from the mountain with the Ten Commandments, which are the code of the old covenant, his face shone with such a splendour that no one could look at it (*Exodus* 34:30). Obviously that was a transient splendour. It did not and it could not last. The new covenant, the new relationship which Jesus Christ makes possible between man and God, has a greater splendour which will never fade because it produces pardon and not condemnation, life and not death.

Here is the warning. The Jews preferred the old covenant, the law; they rejected the new covenant, the new relationship in Christ. Now the old covenant was not a bad thing; but it was only a second-best, a stage upon the way. As a great commentator has put it, "When the sun has risen the lamps cease to be of use." And as has been so truly said, "The second-best is the worst enemy of the best." Men have always tended to cling to the old even when something far better is offered. For long people on so-called religious grounds refused to use chloroform. When Wordsworth and the romantic poets emerged, criticism said, "This will never do." When Wagner began to write his music, people would not have it. Churches all over the world cling to the old and refuse the new. Because a thing was always done, it is right, and because a thing was never done, it is wrong. We must be careful not to worship the stages instead of the goal, not to cling to the second-best while the best is waiting, not, as the Jews did, to insist that the old ways are right and refuse the new glories which God is opening to us.

DAY SEVEN

The Father in Heaven

Matthew 6:9

Our Father in Heaven

(i) If we believe that God is Father, *it settles our relationship to our fellow-men.* If God is Father, he is Father of all men. The Lord's Prayer does not teach us to pray *My Father;* it teaches us to pray *Our Father.*

It is very significant that in the Lord's Prayer the words *I, me* and *mine* never occur; it is true to say that Jesus came to take these words out of life and to put in their place *we, us* and *ours.* God is not any man's exclusive possession. The very phrase *Our Father* involves *the elimination of self.* The fatherhood of God is the only possible basis of the brotherhood of man.

(ii) If we believe that God is Father, *it settles our relationship to ourselves.* There are times when every man despises and hates himself. He knows himself to be lower than the lowest thing that crawls upon the earth. The heart knows its own bitterness, and no one knows a man's unworthiness better than that man himself.

Mark Rutherford wished to add a new beatitude: "Blessed are those who heal us of our self-despisings." Blessed are those who give us back our self-respect. That is precisely what God does. In these grim, bleak, terrible moments we can still remind ourselves that, even if we matter to no one else, we matter to God; that in the infinite mercy of God we are of royal lineage, children of the King of kings.

(iii) If we believe that God is Father, *it settles our relationship to God.* It is not that it removes the might, majesty and power of God. It is not that it makes God any the less God; but it makes that might, and majesty and power, approachable for us.

There is an old Roman story which tells how a Roman Emperor was enjoying a triumph. He had the privilege, which Rome gave to her great victors, of marching his troops through the streets of Rome, with all his captured trophies and his prisoners in his train. So the Emperor was on the march with his troops. The streets were lined with cheering people. The tall legionaries lined the streets' edges to keep the people in their places. At one point on the triumphal route there was a little platform where the Empress and her family were sitting to watch the Emperor go by in all the pride of his triumph. On the platform with his mother there was the Emperor's youngest son, a little boy. As the Emperor came near the little boy jumped off the platform, burrowed through the crowd, tried to dodge between the legs of a legionary, and to run out on to the road to meet his father's chariot. The legionary stooped down and stopped him. He swung him up in his arms: "You can't do that, boy," he said. "Don't you know who that is in the chariot? That's the Emperor. You can't run out to his chariot." And the little lad laughed down. "He may be your Emperor," he said, "but he's my father." That is exactly the way the Christian feels toward God. The might, and the majesty, and the power are the might, and the majesty, and the power of one whom Jesus taught us to call *Our Father.*

DAY EIGHT

On False Pretences

Matthew 7:21–23

Not everyone that says to me: "Lord, Lord" will enter into the Kingdom of Heaven, but he who does the will of my father who is in heaven. Many will say to me on that day: "Lord, Lord, did we not prophesy in your name, and in your name did we not cast out devils, and in your name did we not do many deeds of power?" Then will I publicly announce to them: "I never knew you. Depart from me you doers of iniquity.

There is an apparently surprising feature about this passage. Jesus is quite ready to concede that many of the false prophets will do and say wonderful and impressive things.

We must remember what the ancient world was like. Miracles were common events. The frequency of miracles came from the ancient idea of illness. In the ancient world all illness was held to be the work of demons. A man was ill because a demon had succeeded in exercising some malign influence over him, or in winning a way into some part of his body. Cures were therefore wrought by exorcism. The result of all this was that a great deal of illness was what we would call psychological, as were a great many cures. If a man succeeded in convincing—or deluding—himself into a belief that a demon was in him or had him in his power, that man would undoubtedly be ill. And if someone could convince him that the hold of the demon was broken, then quite certainly that man would be cured.

The leaders of the Church never denied heathen miracles. In answer to the miracles of Christ, Celsus quoted the miracles attributed to Aesculapius and Apollo. Even in the New Testament we read of Jewish exorcists who added the name of Jesus to their repertoire, and who banished devils by its aid (*Acts* 19:13). There was many a charlatan who rendered a lip service to Jesus Christ, and who used his name to produce wonderful effects on demon-possessed people. What Jesus is saying is that if any man uses his name on false pretences, the day of reckoning will come. His real motives will be exposed, and he will be banished from the presence of God.

There are two great permanent truths within this passage. There is only one way in which a man's sincerity can be proved, and that is by his practice. Fine words can never be a substitute for fine deeds. There is only one proof of love, and that proof is obedience. There is no point in saying that we love a person, and then doing things which break that person's heart. When we were young maybe we used sometimes to say to our mothers, "Mother, I love you." And maybe mother sometimes smiled a little wistfully and said, "I wish you would show it a little more in the way you behave." So often we confess God with our lips and deny him with our lives. It is not difficult to recite a creed, but it is difficult to live the Christian life. Faith without practice is a contradiction in terms, and love without obedience is an impossibility.

DAY NINE

The Christian and His Fellow-Men

Romans 12:14–21

Bless those who persecute you; bless them and do not curse them.
Rejoice with those who rejoice, and weep with those who weep.
Live in harmony with one another.
Keep your thoughts from pride; and never refuse to be associated with humble people.
Don't become conceitedly wise in your own estimation.
Never return evil for evil.
Take thought to make your conduct fair for all to see.
If it is possible, as far as you can, live at peace with all men.
Beloved, do not seek to revenge yourself on others; leave such vengeance to The Wrath, for it stands written: "Vengeance belongs to me; I

*will repay, says the Lord." Rather, if your enemy is hungry, give him
food. If he is thirsty, give him drink. If you do this you will heap
coals of fire on his head. Be not overcome by evil, but overcome evil
with good.*

Paul offers a series of rules and principles wherewith to govern our relationships with our fellow-men.

(i) The Christian must meet persecution with a prayer for those
who persecute him. Long ago Plato had said that the good man will
choose rather to suffer evil than to do evil; and it is always evil to hate.
When the Christian is hurt, and insulted, and maltreated, he has the
example of his Master before him, for he, upon his Cross, prayed for
forgiveness for those who were killing him.

There has been no greater force to move men into Christianity
than this serene forgiveness which the martyrs in every age have
showed. Stephen died praying for forgiveness for those who stoned
him to death (*Acts* 7:60). Among those who killed him was a young
man named Saul, who afterward became Paul, the apostle to the Gentiles and the slave of Christ. There can be no doubt that the death
scene of Stephen was one of the things that turned Paul to Christ. As
Augustine said: "The Church owes Paul to the prayer of Stephen."
Many a persecutor has become a follower of the faith he once sought
to destroy, because he has seen how a Christian can forgive.

(ii) We are to rejoice with those who rejoice, and to weep with those
who weep. There are few bonds like that of a common sorrow. A lady
in Charleston met the servant of a neighbour. "I'm sorry to hear of
your Aunt Lucy's death," she said. "You must miss her greatly. You were
such friends." "Yes," said the servant, "I am sorry she died. But we
weren't friends." "Why," said the lady, "I thought you were. I've seen
you laughing and talking together lots of times." "Yes. That's so," came
the reply. "We've laughed together, and we've talked together, but we
were just acquaintances. You see, Miss Ruth, we never shed any tears.
Folks have to cry together before they are friends."

The bond of tears is the strongest of all. And yet it is much easier
to weep with those who weep than it is to rejoice with those who rejoice. Long ago Chrysostom wrote on this passage: "It requires more

of a high Christian temper to rejoice with them that do rejoice than to weep with them that weep. For this nature itself fulfils perfectly; and there is none so hard-hearted as not to weep over him that is in calamity; but the other requires a very noble soul, so as not only to keep from envying, but even to feel pleasure with the person who is in esteem." It is, indeed, more difficult to congratulate another on his success, especially if his success involves disappointment to us, than it is to sympathize with his sorrow and his loss. It is only when self is dead that we can take as much joy in the success of others as in our own.

(iii) We are to live in harmony with one another. It was Nelson who, after one of his great victories, sent back a despatch in which he gave us the reason for it: "I had the happiness to command a band of brothers." It is a band of brothers that any Christian Church should be. Leighton once wrote: "The mode of Church government is unconstrained; but peace and concord, kindness and good will are indispensable." When strife enters into any Christian society, the hope of doing any good work is gone.

(iv) We are to avoid all pride and snobbishness. We have always to remember that the standards by which the world judges a man are not necessarily the standards by which God judges him. Saintliness has nothing to do with rank, or wealth, or birth. Dr James Black in his own vivid way described a scene in an early Christian congregation. A notable convert has been made, and the great man comes to his first Church service. He enters the room where the service is being held. The Christian leader points to a place. "Will you sit there please?" "But," says the man, "I cannot sit there, for that would be to sit beside my slave." "Will you sit there please?" repeats the leader. "But," says the man, "surely not beside my slave." "Will you sit there please?" repeats the leader once again. And the man at last crosses the room, sits beside his slave and gives him the kiss of peace. That is what Christianity did; and that is what it alone could do in the Roman Empire. The Christian Church was the only place where master and slave sat side by side. It is still the place where all earthly distinctions are gone, for with God there is no respect of persons.

(v) We are to make our conduct fair for all to see. Paul was well aware that Christian conduct must not only be good; it must also look good.

So-called Christianity can be presented in the hardest and most unlovely way; but real Christianity is something which is fair for all to see.

(vi) We are to live at peace with all men. But Paul adds two qualifications. (*a*) He says, *if it be possible.* There may come a time when the claims of courtesy have to submit to the claims of principle. Christianity is not an easy-going tolerance which will accept anything and shut its eyes to everything. There may come a time when some battle has to be fought, and when it does, the Christian will not shirk it. (*b*) He says, *as far as you can.* Paul knew very well that it is easier for some to live at peace than for others. He knew that one man can be compelled to control as much temper in an hour as another man in a lifetime. We would do well to remember that goodness is a great deal easier for some than for others; that will keep us alike from criticism and from discouragement.

(vii) We are to keep ourselves from all thought of taking revenge. Paul gives three reasons for that. (*a*) Vengeance does not belong to us but to God. In the last analysis no human being has a right to judge any other; only God can do that. (*b*) To treat a man with kindness rather than vengeance is the way to move him. Vengeance may break his spirit; but kindness will break his heart. "If we are kind to our enemies," says Paul, "it will heap coals of fire on their heads." That means, not that it will store up further punishment for them, but that it will move them to burning shame. (*c*) To stoop to vengeance is to be ourselves conquered by evil. Evil can never be conquered by evil. If hatred is met with more hatred it is only increased; but if it is met with love, an antidote for the poison is found. As Booker Washington said: "I will not allow any man to make me lower myself by hating him." The only real way to destroy an enemy is to make him a friend.

DAY TEN

The Only True Foundation

Matthew 7:24–27

So, then, everyone who hears these words of mine and does them will be likened to a wise man who built his house upon the rock. And the rain came down, and the rivers swelled, and the wind blew, and fell upon that house, and it did not fall, for it was founded upon the rock. And everyone who hears these words of mine and does not do them will be likened to a foolish man who built his house upon the sand. And the rain came down, and the rivers swelled, and the winds blew and bear upon that house, and it fell; and its fall was great.

And when Jesus had ended these words, the people were astonished at his teaching, for he was teaching them as one who had authority, and not as their Scribes.

Jesus was in a double sense an expert. He was an expert in scripture. The writer of *Proverbs* gave him the hint for his picture: "When the tempest passes, the wicked is no more, but the righteous is established for ever" (*Proverbs* 10:25). Here is the germ of the picture which Jesus drew of the two houses and the two builders. But Jesus was also an expert in life. He was the craftsman who knew all about the building of houses, and when he spoke about the foundations of a house he knew what he was talking about. This is no illustration formed by a scholar in his study; this is the illustration of a practical man.

Nor is this a far-fetched illustration; it is a story of the kind of thing which could well happen. In Palestine the builder must think ahead. There was many a gully which in summer was a pleasant sandy hollow, but was in winter a raging torrent of rushing water. A man might be looking for a house; he might find a pleasantly sheltered sandy hollow; and he might think this a very suitable place. But, if he was a short-sighted man, he might well have built his house in the dried-up bed of a river, and when the winter came, his house would disintegrate. Even on an ordinary site it was tempting to begin building on the smoothed-over sand, and not to bother digging down to the shelf of rock below, but that way disaster lay ahead.

Only a house whose foundations are firm can withstand the storm; and only a life whose foundations are sure can stand the test. Jesus demanded two things.

(i) He demanded that men should *listen.* One of the great difficulties which face us today is the simple fact that men often do not know what Jesus said or what the Church teaches. In fact the matter is worse. They have often a quite mistaken notion of what Jesus said and of what the Church teaches. It is no part of the duty of an honorable man to condemn either a person, or an institution, unheard—and that today is precisely what so many do. The first step to the Christian life is simply to give Jesus Christ a chance to be heard.

(ii) He demanded that men should *do*. Knowledge only becomes relevant when it is translated into action. It would be perfectly possible for a man to pass an examination in Christian Ethics with the highest distinction, and yet not to be a Christian. Knowledge must become action; theory must become practice; theology must become life. There is little point in going to a doctor, unless we are prepared to do the things we hear him say to us. There is little point in going to an expert, unless we are prepared to act upon his advice. And yet there are thousands of people who listen to the teaching of Jesus Christ every Sunday, and who have a very good knowledge of what Jesus taught, and who yet make little or no deliberate attempt to put it into practice. If we are to be in any sense followers of Jesus we must *hear* and *do*.

Is there any word in which *hearing* and *doing* are summed up? There is such a word, and that word is obedience. Jesus demands our implicit *obedience*. To learn to obey is the most important thing in life.

Some time ago there was a report of the case of a sailor in the Royal Navy who was very severely punished for a breach of discipline. So severe was the punishment that in certain civilian quarters it was thought to be far too severe. A newspaper asked its readers to express their opinions about the severity of the punishment.

One who answered was a man who himself had served for years in the Royal Navy. In his view the punishment was not too severe. He held that discipline was absolutely essential, for the purpose of discipline was to condition a man automatically and unquestioningly to obey orders, and on such obedience a man's life might well depend. He cited a case from his own experience. He was in a launch which was towing a much heavier vessel in a rough sea. The vessel was attached to the launch by a wire hawser. Suddenly in the midst of the wind and the spray there came a single, insistent word of command from the officer in charge of the launch. "Down!" he shouted. On the spot the crew of the launch flung themselves down. Just at that moment the wire towing-hawser snapped, and the broken parts of it whipped about like a maddened steel snake. If any man had been struck by it he would have been instantly killed. But the whole crew automatically obeyed and no one was injured. If anyone had stopped to argue, or to ask why, he would have been a dead man. Obedience saved lives.

It is such obedience that Jesus demands. It is Jesus' claim that obedience to him is the only sure foundation for life; and it is his promise that the life which is founded on obedience to him is safe, no matter what storms may come.

DAY ELEVEN

The Golden Rule of Jesus

Matthew 7:12
So, then, all the things which you wish that men should do to you, so do you do to Them; for this is the Law and the prophets.

Let us see just how the positive form of the golden rule differs from the negative form; and let us see just how much more Jesus was demanding than any teacher had ever demanded before.

When this rule is put in its negative form, when we are told that we must refrain from doing to others that which we would not wish them to do to us, it is not an essentially religious rule at all. It is simply a common-sense statement without which no social intercourse at all would be possible. Sir Thomas Browne once said, "We are beholden to every man we meet that he doth not kill us." In a sense that is true, but, if we could not assume that the conduct and the behaviour of other people to us would conform to the accepted standards of civilized life, then life would be intolerable. The negative form of the golden rule is not in any sense an extra; it is something without which life could not go on at all.

Further, the negative form of the rule involves nothing more than *not* doing certain things; it means refraining from certain actions. It is never very difficult *not* to do things. That we must not do injury to other people is not a specially religious principle; it is rather a legal principle. It is the kind of principle that could well be kept by a man who has no belief and no interest in religion at all. A man might for-ever refrain from doing any injury to anyone else, and yet be a quite useless citizen to his fellow-men. A man could satisfy the negative form of the rule by simple inaction; if he consistently did nothing he would never break it. And a goodness which consists in doing nothing would be a contradiction of everything that Christian goodness means.

When this rule is put positively, when we are told that we must ac-tively do to others what we would have them do to us, a new princi-ple enters into life, and a new attitude to our fellow-men. It is one thing to say, "I must not injure people; I must not do to them what I would object to their doing to me." That, the law can compel us to do. It is quite another thing to say, "I must go out of my way to help other people and to be kind to them, as I would wish them to help and to be kind to me." That, only love can compel us to do. The at-titude which says, "I must do no harm to people," is quite different from the attitude which says, "I must do my best to help people."

To take a very simple analogy—if a man has a motor car the law can compel him to drive it in such a way that he does not injure any-one else on the road, but no law can compel him to stop and to give a weary and a foot-sore traveler a lift along the road. It is quite sim-ple thing to refrain from hurting and injuring people; it is not so very difficult to respect their principles and their feelings; it is a far harder thing to make it the chosen and deliberate policy of life to go out of our way to be as kind to them as we would wish them to be to us.

And yet it is just that new attitude which makes life beautiful. Jane Stoddart quotes an incident from the life of W. H. Smith. "When Smith was at the War Office, his private secretary, Mr. Fleetwood Wil-son, noticed that at the end of a week's work, when his chief was preparing to leave for Greenlands on a Saturday afternoon, he used to pack a despatch-box with the papers he required to take with him, and carry it himself on his journey. Mr. Wilson remarked that Mr.

Smith would save himself much trouble, if he did as was the practice of other ministers—leave the papers to be put in an office 'pouch' and sent by post. Mr. Smith looked rather ashamed for a moment, and then looking up at his secretary said, 'Well, my dear Wilson, that fact is this: our postman who brings the letters from Henley has plenty to carry. I watched him one morning coming up the approach with my heavy pouch in addition to his usual load, and I determined to save him as much as I could.' " An action like that shows a certain attitude to one's fellow-men. It is the attitude which believes that we should treat our fellow-men, not as the law allows, but as love demands.

It is perfectly possible for a man of the world to observe the negative form of the golden rule. He could without very serious difficulty so discipline his life that he would not do to others what he did not wish them to do to him; but the only man who can even begin to satisfy the positive form of the rule is the man who has the love of Christ within his heart. He will try to forgive as he would wish to be forgiven, to help as he would wish to be helped, to praise as he would wish to be praised, to understand as he would wish to be understood. He will never seek to avoid doing things; he will always look for things to do. Clearly this will make life much more complicated; clearly he will have much less time to spend on his own desires and his own activities, for time and time again he will have to stop what he is doing to help someone else. It will be a principle which will dominate his life at home, in the factory, in the bus, in the office, in the street, in the train, at his games, everywhere. He can never do it until self withers and dies within his heart. To obey this commandment a man must become a new man with a new center to his life; and if the world was composed of people who sought to obey this rule, it would be a new world.

DAY TWELVE

The Charter of Prayer

Matthew 7:7–11

Keep on asking, and it will be given you;
Keep on seeking, and you will find;

Keep on knocking, and it will be opened to you.
For everyone that asks receives;
And he who seeks finds;
And to him who knocks it will be opened.
What man is there, who, if his son will ask him for bread, will give
him a stone? Or, if he will ask for a fish, will he give him a serpent?
If, then, you, who are grudging, know how to give good gifts to your
children, how much more will your Father in heaven give good
things to them that ask him?

Any man who prays is bound to want to know to what kind of God he is praying. He wants to know in what kind of atmosphere his prayers will be heard. Is he praying to a grudging God out of whom every gift has to be squeezed and coerced? Is he praying to a mocking God whose gifts may well be double-edged? Is he praying to a God whose heart is so kind that he is more ready to give than we are to ask?

Jesus came from a nation which loved prayer. The Jewish Rabbis said the loveliest things about prayer. "God is near to his creatures as the ear to the mouth." "Human beings can hardly hear two people talking at once, but God, if all the world calls to him at the one time, hears their cry." "A man is annoyed by being worried by the requests of his friends, but with God, all the time a man puts his needs and requests before him, God loves him all the more." Jesus had been brought up to love prayer; and in this passage he gives us the Christian charter of prayer.

Jesus' argument is very simple. One of the Jewish Rabbis asked, "Is there a man who ever hates his son?" Jesus' argument is that no father ever refused the request of his son; and God the great Father will never refuse the requests of his children.

Jesus' examples are carefully chosen. He takes three examples, for *Luke* adds a third to the two *Matthew* gives. If a son asks for bread, will his father give him a stone? If a son asks for a fish, will his father give him a serpent? If a son asks for an egg, will his father give him a scorpion? (*Luke* 11:12.) The point is that in each case the two things cited bear a close resemblance.

The little, round, limestone stones on the seashore were exactly the shape and the color of little loaves. If a son asks for bread will his father mock him by offering him a stone, which looks like bread but which is impossible to eat?

If a son asks for a fish, will his father give him a serpent? Almost certainly the *serpent* is an *eel.* According to the Jewish food laws an eel could not be eaten, because an eel was an unclean fish. "Everything in the waters that has not fins and scales is an abomination to you" (*Leviticus* 11:12). That regulation ruled out the eel as an article of diet. If a son asks for a fish, will his father indeed give him a fish, but a fish which it is forbidden to eat, and which is useless to eat? Would a father mock his son's hunger like that?

If the son asks for an egg, will his father give him a scorpion? The scorpion is a dangerous little animal. In action it is rather like a small lobster, with claws with which it clutches its victim. Its sting is in its tail, and it brings its tail up over its back to strike its victim. The sting can be exceedingly painful, and sometimes even fatal. When the scorpion is at rest its claws and tail are folded in, and there is a pale kind of scorpion, which, when folded up, would look exactly like an egg. If a son asks for an egg, will his father mock him by handing him a biting scorpion?

God will never refuse our prayers; and God will never mock our prayers. The Greeks had their stories about the gods who answered men's prayers, but the answer was an answer with a barb in it, a double-edged gift. Aurora, the goddess of the dawn, fell in love with Tithonus, a mortal youth, so the Greek story ran. Zeus, the king of the gods, offered her any gift that she might choose for her mortal lover. Aurora very naturally chose that Tithonus might live forever; but she had forgotten to ask that Tithonus might remain forever young; and so Tithonus grew older and older and older, and could never die, and the gift became a curse.

There is a lesson here; God will always answer our prayers; *but he will answer them in his way,* and his way will be the way of perfect wisdom and of perfect love. Often if he answered our prayers as we at the moment desired it would be the worst thing possible for us, for in our ignorance we often ask for gifts which would be our ruin. This saying of Jesus tells us, not only that God will answer, but that God will answer in wisdom and in love.

Although this is the charter of prayer, it lays certain obligations upon us. In Greek there are two kinds of imperative; there is the *aorist* imperative which issues one definite command. "Shut the door behind you" would be an *aorist* imperative. There is the *present* imperative which issues a command that a man should always do something or should go on doing something. "Always shut doors behind you" would be a present imperative. The imperatives here are *present* imperatives; therefore Jesus is saying, "Go on asking; go on seeking; go on knocking." He is telling us to persist in prayer; he is telling us never to be discouraged in prayer. Clearly therein lies the test of our sincerity. Do we really want a thing? Is a thing such that we can bring it repeatedly into the presence of God, for the biggest test of any desire is: Can I pray about it?

Jesus here lays down the twin facts that God will always answer our prayers *in his way,* in wisdom and in love; and that we must bring to God an undiscouraged life of prayer, which tests the rightness of the things we pray for, and which tests our own sincerity in asking for them.

DAY THIRTEEN

The Supremacy of Love

1 Corinthians 13:8–13

Love never fails. Whatever prophecies there are, they will vanish away. Whatever tongues there are, they will cease. Whatever knowledge we have, it will pass away. It is only part of the truth that we know now and only part of the truth that we can forthtell to others. But when that which is complete shall come, that which is incomplete will vanish away. When I was a child I used to speak like a child. When I became a man I put an end to childish things. Now we see only reflections in a mirror which leave us with nothing but riddles to solve, but then we shall see face to face. Now I know in part; but then I will know even as I am known. Now faith, hope, love remain—these three; but the greatest of these is love.

In verses 8–13 Paul has three final things to say of this Christian love.

(i) He stresses its *absolute permanency*. When all the things in which men glory have passed away love will still stand. In one of the most wonderfully lyrical verses of scripture *The Song of Solomon* (8:7) sings, "Many waters cannot quench love, neither can floods drown it." The one unconquerable thing is love. That is one of the great reasons for believing in immortality. When love is entered into, there comes into life a relationship against which the assaults of time are helpless and which transcends death.

(ii) He stresses its *absolute completeness*. As things are, what we see are reflections in a mirror. That would be even more suggestive to the Corinthians than it is to us. Corinth was famous for its manufacture of mirrors. But the modern mirror as we know it, with its perfect reflection, did not emerge until the thirteenth century. The Corinthian mirror was made of highly polished metal and, even at its best, gave but an imperfect reflection. It has been suggested that what this phrase means is that we see as through a window made with horn. In those days windows were so made and all that could be seen through them was a dim and shadow outline. In fact the Rabbis had a saying that it was through such a window that Moses saw God.

In this life Paul feels we see only the reflections of God and are left with much that is mystery and riddle. We see that reflection in God's world, for the work of anyone's hands tells us something about the workman; we see it in the Gospel and we see it in Jesus Christ. Even if in Christ we have the perfect revelation, our seeking minds can grasp it only in part, for the finite can never grasp the infinite. Our knowledge is still like the knowledge of a child. But the way of love will lead us in the end to a day when the veil is drawn aside and we see face to face and know even as we are known. We cannot ever reach that day without love, because God is love and only he who loves can see him.

(iii) He stresses its *absolute supremacy*. Great as faith and hope are, love is still greater. Faith without love is cold, and hope without love is grim. Love is the fire which kindles faith and it is the light which turns hope into certainty.

DAY FOURTEEN

Faith and Its Secret

Hebrews 11:23–29

It was faith that Moses, when he was born, was kept hidden for three months by his parents, because they saw that the child was beautiful: and they did not fear the edict of the king. It was by faith that Moses, when he grew to manhood, refused to be called the son of Pharaoh's daughter and chose rather to suffer evil with the people of God than to enjoy the transient pleasure of sin, for he considered that a life of reproach for the sake of the Messiah was greater wealth than the treasure of Egypt, for he kept his eyes fixed upon his reward. It was by faith that he left Egypt, unmoved by the blazing anger of the king, for he could face all things as one who sees him who is invisible. It was by faith that he carried out the Passover and the sprinkling of blood, so that the destroying angel might not touch the children of his people. It was by faith that they crossed the Red Sea as if they were going through dry land and that the Egyptians, when they ventured to try to do so, were engulfed.

To the Hebrews Moses was the supreme figure in their history. He was the leader who had rescued them from slavery and who had received the Law of their lives from God. To the writer of the letter to the Hebrews Moses was preeminently the man of faith. In this story, as Moffatt points out, there are five different acts of faith. As with the other great characters whose names are included in this roll of honour of God's faithful ones, many legends and elaborations had gathered round the name of Moses and doubtless the writer of this letter had them also in his mind.

(i) There was the faith of Moses' parents. The story of their action is told in *Exodus* 2:1–10. *Exodus* 1:15–22 tells how the king of Egypt in his hatred tried to wipe out the children of the Israelites by having them killed at birth. Legend tells how Amram and Jochebed, the parents of Moses (*Exodus* 6:20), were troubled by the decree of Pharaoh. As a result Amram put away his wife, not because he did not love her, but because he would spare her the sorrow of seeing her children killed. For three years she was put away, and then Miriam prophesied: "My parents shall have another son, who shall deliver Israel out of the hands of the Egyptians." She said to her father: "What hast thou done? Thou hast sent thy wife away out of thine house, because thou couldst not trust the Lord God that he would protect the child that might be born to thee." So Amram, shamed into trusting God, took back his wife; and in due time Moses was born. He was so lovely a child that his parents determined to hide him in their house. This they did for three months. Then, the legend tells, the Egyptians struck upon a cruel scheme. The king was determined that hidden children should be sought out and killed. Now when a child hears another child cry, he will cry too. So Egyptian mothers were sent into the homes of the Israelites with their babies; there they pricked their babies until they cried. This made the hidden children of the Israelites cry, too, and so they were discovered and killed. In view of this, Amram and Jochebed decided to make a little ark and to entrust their child to it on the waters of the Nile.

That Moses was born at all was an act of faith; that he was preserved was another. He began by being the child of faith.

(ii) The second act of faith was Moses' loyalty to his own people. The story is told in *Exodus* 2:11–14. Again the legends help to light up the picture. When Moses was entrusted to the waters of the Nile, he was found by the daughter of Pharaoh, whose name is given as Bithia, or more commonly Thermouthis. She was entranced by his beauty. Legend says that when she drew the ark out of the water, the archangel Gabriel boxed the ears of the little baby to make him cry so that the heart of Thermouthis might be touched as she saw the little face puckered in sorrow and the eyes full of tears. Thermouthis, much to her sorrow, was childless; so she took the baby Moses home, and cared for him as her own son. He grew to be so beautiful that people turned in the street, and even ceased their work, to look at him. He was so wise that he was far beyond all other children in learning and in knowledge. When he was still a child, Thermouthis took him to Pharaoh and told him how she had found him. She placed him in his arms, and he was so entranced by the child that he embraced him and, at the request of Thermouthis, he promised to make him his heir.

So Moses was spared. He was brought up in all luxury. He was heir to the kingdom. He became one of the greatest of all Egyptian generals; in particular he conquered the Ethiopians when they were threatening Egypt and in the end was married to an Ethiopian princess. But all the time he had never forgotten his fellow-countrymen; and the day came when he decided to ally himself with the downtrodden Israelites and say goodbye to the future of riches and royalty that he might have had.

Moses gave up earthly glory for the sake of the people of God. Christ gave up his glory for the sake of mankind and accepted scourging and shame and a terrible death. Moses in his day and generation shared in the sufferings of Christ, choosing the loyalty that led to suffering rather than the ease which led to earthly glory. He knew that the prizes of earth were contemptible compared with the ultimate reward of God.

(iii) There came the day when Moses, because of his intervention on behalf of his people, had to withdraw from Egypt to Midian (*Exodus* 2:14–22). Because of the order in which it comes that must be what verse 27 refers to. Some people have found difficulty here, because the Exodus narrative says that it was because Moses feared Pharaoh that he fled to Midian (*Exodus* 2:14), while Hebrews says that he went out not fearing the blazing wrath of the king. There is no real contradiction. It is simply that the writer of the letter to the Hebrews saw even more deeply into the story. For Moses to withdraw to Midian was not an act of fear; it was an act of courage. It showed the courage of the man who has learned to wait.

The Stoics were wise; they held that a man should not throw his life away by needlessly provoking the wrath of a tyrant. Seneca wrote: "The wise man will never provoke the wrath of mighty men; nay, he will turn aside from it; in just the same way as sailors in sailing will not deliberately court the danger of the storm." At that moment Moses might have gone on but his people were not ready. If he had gone on recklessly he would simply have thrown his life away and the deliverance from Egypt might never have happened. He was big enough and brave enough to wait until God said: "Now is the hour."

Moffatt quotes a saying of A. S. Peake: "The courage to abandon work on which one's heart is set and accept inaction cheerfully as the will of God is of the rarest and highest kind and can be created and sustained only by the clearest spiritual vision." When our fighting instincts say: "Go on," it takes a big and a brave man to wait. It is human to fear to miss the chance; but it is great to wait for the time of God—even when it seems like throwing a chance away.

(iv) There came the day when Moses had to make all the arrangements for the first Passover. The account is in *Exodus* 12:12–48. The unleavened bread had to be made; the Passover lamb had to be slain; the doorpost had to be smeared with the blood of the lamb so that the Angel of Death would see the blood and pass over that house and not slay the firstborn in it. But the really amazing thing is that, according to the Exodus story, Moses not only made these regulations for the night on which the children of Israel were leaving Israel; he also laid it down that *they were to be observed annually for all time.* That is to say, he never doubted the success of the enterprise, never doubted that the people would be delivered from Egypt and that some day they would reach the promised land. Here was a band of wretched Hebrew slaves about to set off on a journey across an unknown desert to an unknown promised land and here was the whole power of Egypt hot upon their heels; yet Moses never doubted that God would bring them safely through. He was preeminently the man who had the faith that if God gave his people an order he would also give them the strength to carry it out. Moses knew well that God does not summon his servants to a great task and leave it at that; he goes with them every step of the way.

(v) There was the great act of the crossing of the Red Sea. The story is told in *Exodus* 14. There we read of how the children of Israel were wondrously enabled to pass through and of how the Egyptians were engulfed when they tried to do the same. It was at that moment that the faith of Moses communicated itself to the people and drove them on when they might well have turned back. Here we have the faith of a leader and of a people who were prepared to attempt the impossible at the command of God, realizing that the greatest barrier in the world is no barrier if God be there to help us overpass it. The book *As in Adam* has this sentence: "The business of life, the way to life, consists in getting over fences, not in lying down and moaning on the hither side." To Moses belonged the faith to attempt what appeared to be the most insurmountable fences in the certainty that God would help the man who refused to turn back and insisted on going on.

Finally, this passage not only tells us of the faith of Moses; it also tells us of *the source of that faith*. Verse 27 tells us that he was able to face all things as one who sees him who is invisible. The outstanding characteristic of Moses was the close intimacy of his relationship with God. In *Exodus* 33:9–11 we read of how he went into the Tabernacle: "and the Lord used to speak to Moses face to face, as a man speaks to his friend." In *Numbers* 12:7, 8 we read of God's verdict on him when there were those who were ready to rebel against him: "with him I speak mouth to mouth." To put it simply—the secret of his faith was that Moses knew God personally. To every task he came out from God's presence.

It is told that before a great battle Napoleon would stand in his tent alone; he would send for his commanders to come to him, one by one; when they came in, he would say no word but would look them in the eye and shake them by the hand; and they would go out prepared to die for the general whom they loved. That is like Moses and God. Moses had the faith he had because he knew God in the way he did. When we come to it straight from God's presence, no task can ever defeat us. Our failure and our fear are so often due to the fact that we try to do things alone. The secret of victorious living is to face God before we face men.

DAY FIFTEEN

Each Man a Letter of Christ

2 Corinthians 3:1–3

Are we beginning to commend ourselves again? Surely you do not think that we need—as some people need—letters of commendation either to

you or from you? You are our letter, written on our hearts, known and
read by all men. It is plain to see that you are a letter written by Christ,
produced under our ministry, written not with ink, but with the Spirit
of the living God, not on tablets of stone, but on tablets which are living,
beating, human hearts.

Behind this passage lies the thought of a custom which was common
in the ancient world, that of sending letters of commendation with a
person. If someone was going to a strange community, a friend of his
who knew someone in that community would give him a letter of
commendation to introduce him and to testify to his character.

Here is such a letter, found among the papyri, written by a certain
Aurelius Archelaus, who was a *beneficiarius*—that is, a soldier privi-
leged to have special exemption from all menial duties—to his com-
manding officer, a military tribune called Julius Domitius. It is to introduce and commend a certain Theon. "To Julius Domitius, military
tribune of the legion, from Aurelius Archelaus, his *beneficiarius,* greet-
ing. I have already before this recommended to you Theon, my
friend, and now also, I ask you, sir, to have him before your eyes as
you would myself. For he is a man such as to deserve to be loved by
you, for he left his own people, his goods and his business and followed me, and through all things he has kept me safe. I therefore pray
you that he may have the right to come and see you. He can tell you
everything about our business. . . . I have loved the man. . . . I wish
you, sir, great happiness and long life with your family and good
health. Have this letter before your eyes and let it make you think that
I am speaking to you. Farewell."

That was the kind of commendatory letter, or reference, of which
Paul was thinking. There is one such in the New Testament. *Romans*
16 is a letter of commendation written to introduce Phoebe, a member of the Church at Cenchrea, to the Church at Rome.

In the ancient world, as nowadays, sometimes written testimoni-
als did not mean very much. A man once asked Diogenes, the Cynic
philosopher, for such a letter. Diogenes answered, "That you are a
man he will know at a glance; but whether you are a good or a bad

man he will discover if he has the skill to distinguish between good and bad, and if he is without that skill he will not discover the facts even though I write to him thousands of times." Yet in the Christian Church such letters were necessary, for even Lucian, the pagan satirist, noted that any charlatan could make a fortune out of the simple-minded Christians, because they were so easily imposed upon.

The previous sentences of Paul's letter seemed to read as if he was giving himself a testimonial. He declares that he has no need of such commendation. Then he takes a side-glance at those who have been causing trouble in Corinth. "There may be some," he says, "who brought you letters of commendation or who got them from you." In all probability these were emissaries of the Jews who had come to undo Paul's work and who had brought introductory letters from the Sanhedrin to accredit them. Once Paul had had such letters himself, when he set out to Damascus to obliterate the Church (*Acts* 9:2). He says that his only testimonial is the Corinthians themselves. The change in their character and life is the only commendation that he needs.

He goes on to make a great claim. Every one of them is a letter of Christ. Long ago Plato had said that the good teacher does not write his message in ink that will fade; he writes it upon men. That is what Jesus had done. He had written his message on the Corinthians, through his servant, Paul, not with fading ink but with the Spirit, not on tablets of stone as the law was first written, but on the hearts of men.

There is a great truth here, which is at once an inspiration and an awful warning—every man is an open letter for Jesus Christ. Every Christian, whether he likes it or not, is an advertisement for Christianity. The honour of Christ is in the hands of his followers. We judge a shopkeeper by the kind of goods he sells; we judge a crafts-man by the kind of articles he produces; we judge a Church by the kind of men it creates; and therefore men judge Christ by his follow-ers. Dick Sheppard, after years of talking in the open air to people who were outside the Church, declared that he had discovered that "the greatest handicap the Church has is the unsatisfactory lives of professing Christians." When we go out into the world, we have the awe-inspiring responsibility of being open letters, advertisements, for Christ and his Church.

DAY SIXTEEN

The King's Messenger's Freedom from Fear

Matthew 10:26–31

"Do not fear them; for there is nothing which is covered which shall not be unveiled, and there is nothing hidden which shall not be known. What I tell you in the darkness, speak in the light. What you hear whispered in your ear, proclaim on the housetops. Do not fear those who can kill the body, but who cannot kill the soul. Rather fear him who is able to destroy both soul and body in Gehenna. Are two sparrows not sold for a penny, and not one of them shall light on the ground without your Father's knowledge? The hairs of your head are all numbered. So then do not be afraid; you are of more value than many sparrows."

Three times in this short passage Jesus bids his disciples not to be afraid. In the King's messenger there must be a certain courageous fearlessness which marks him out from other men.

(i) The first commandment is in verses 26, 27, and it speaks of a double fearlessness.

(*a*) They are not to be afraid because there is nothing covered that will not be unveiled, and nothing hidden which will not be known. The meaning of that is that *the truth will triumph.* "Great is the truth," ran the Latin proverb, "and the truth will prevail." When James the Sixth threatened to hang or exile Andrew Melville, Melville's answer was: "You cannot hang or exile the truth." When the Christian is involved in suffering and sacrifice and even martyrdom for his faith, he must remember that the day will come when things will be seen as they really are; and then the power of the persecutor and the heroism of Christian witness will be seen at their true value, and each will have its true reward.

(*b*) They are not to be afraid to speak with boldness the message they have received. What Jesus has told them, they must tell to men.

Here in this one verse (verse 27) lies the true function of the preacher.

First, the preacher must *listen;* he must be in the secret place with Christ, that in the dark hours Christ may speak to him, and that in the loneliness Christ may whisper in his ear. No man can speak for Christ unless Christ has spoken to him; no man can proclaim the truth unless he has listened to the truth; for no man can tell that which he does not know.

In the great days in which the Reformation was coming to birth, Colet invited Erasmus to come to Oxford to give a series of lectures on Moses or Isaiah; but Erasmus knew he was not ready. He wrote back: "But I who have learned to live with myself, and know how scanty my equipment is, can neither claim the learning required for such a task, nor do I think that I possess the strength of mind to sustain the jealousy of so many men, who would be eager to maintain their own ground. The campaign is one that demands, not a tyro, but a practiced general. Neither should you call me immodest in declining a position which it would be most immodest to accept. You are not acting wisely, Colet, in demanding water from a pumice stone, as Plautus said. With what effrontery shall I teach what I have never learned? How am I to warm the coldness of others, when I am shivering myself?"

He who would teach and preach must first in the secret place listen and learn.

Second, the preacher must speak what he has heard from Christ, and he must speak even if his speaking is to gain him the hatred of men, and even if by speaking, he takes his life in his hands.

Men do not like the truth, for, as Diogenes said, truth is like the light to sore eyes. Once Latimer was preaching when Henry the king was present. He knew that he was about to say something which the king would not relish. So in the pulpit he soliloquized aloud with himself. "Latimer! Latimer! Latimer!" he said, "be careful what you say. Henry the king is here." He paused, and then he said, "Latimer! Latimer! Latimer! Be careful what you say. The King of kings is here."

The man with a message speaks to men, but he speaks in the presence of God. It was said of John Knox, as they buried him, "Here lies one who feared God so much that he never feared the face of any man."

The Christian witness is the man who knows no fear, because he knows that the judgments of eternity will correct the judgments of time. The Christian preacher and teacher is the man who listens with reverence and who speaks with courage, because he knows that, whether he listens or speaks, he is in the presence of God.

DAY SEVENTEEN

Tribulation and Triumph

2 Corinthians 4:7–15

But we have this treasure in earthen vessels, so that the power which surpasses all things may be seen to be of God and not of us. We are sore pressed at every point, but not hemmed in. We are at our wit's end, but never at our hope's end. We are persecuted by men, but never abandoned by God. We are knocked down, but not knocked out. In our bodies we have to run the same risk of death as Jesus Christ did, so that in our body the same life as Jesus lived may be clear for all to see. For all through our lives we are continually handed over to death for Jesus' sake, so that the life also which Jesus gives may be clear for all to see in our mortal flesh. The result is that death operates in us, but life operates in you. Because we have the same spirit of faith as appears in that passage of scripture where it stands written, "I have believed and therefore have I spoken," we, too, believe and therefore speak, for we know that he who raised up the Lord Jesus will raise us up also with Jesus, and will present us with you. Everything that happens to us is for your sake, so that grace may abound more and more, and so swell the thanksgiving which rises from many to the glory of God.

Paul begins this passage with the thought that it might well be that the privileges which a Christian enjoys might move him to pride. But life is designed to keep a man from pride. However great his Christian glory he is still a mortal man; still the victim of circumstances; still subject to the chances and the changes of human life; still a mortal body with all that body's weakness and pain. He is like a man with a precious treasure contained in an earthen vessel, which itself is weak and worthless. We talk a great deal about the power of man and about the vast forces which he now controls. But the real characteristic of man is not his power but his weakness. As Pascal said, "A drop of water or a breath of air can kill him."

We have already seen what a proud and glorious thing a triumph was for a Roman general. But there were two things designed to keep the general from pride. First, as he rode in the chariot with the crown held over his head, the populace not only shouted their applause but also, ever and again, they shouted, "Look behind you and remember you will die." Second, at the very end of the procession there came the conquering general's own soldiers, and they did two things as they marched. They sang songs in the general's praise, but they also shouted ribald jests and insults to keep him from too much pride.

Life has surrounded us with infirmity, although Christ has surrounded us with glory, so that we may remember that the infirmity is ours and the glory is God's, and recognize our own utter dependence on him.

Paul goes on to describe this Christian life, in which our infirmity is intermingled with God's glory, in a series of paradoxes.

(i) We are sore pressed at every point but not hemmed in. There are all kinds of pressure on us, but we are never in so tight a corner that there is no way out. It is characteristic of the Christian that, even if his body be confined in some difficult environment or some narrow circumstance, there is always an escape route for his spirit to the spaciousness of God.

(ii) We are persecuted by men but never abandoned by God. One of the most notable things about the martyrs is that it was amidst their sorest times that they had their sweetest times with Christ. As Joan of Arc said when she was abandoned by those who should have stood by her, "It is better to be alone with God. His friendship will not fail me, nor his counsel, nor his love. In his strength, I will dare and dare and dare until I die." As the psalmist wrote, "When my father and my mother forsake me, then the Lord will take me up" (*Psalm* 27:10). Nothing can alter the loyalty of God.

(iii) We are at our wit's end but never at our hope's end. There are times when the Christian does not know what is to be done, but even then he never doubts that something *can* be done. There are times when he cannot well see where life is going, but he never doubts that it is going somewhere. If he must "stoop into a dark, tremendous sea of cloud," he still knows that he will emerge. There are times when a Christian has to learn the hardest lesson of all, the very lesson which Jesus himself had to learn in Gethsemane—how to accept what he cannot understand and still to say, "God, Thou art love; I build my faith on that."

Francis Thompson wrote of the presence of Christ on the darkest days:

> But (when so sad thou canst not sadder)
> Cry—and upon thy so sore loss
> Shall shine the traffic of Jacob's ladder
> Pitched betwixt heaven and Charing Cross.
>
> Yea, in the night, my soul, my daughter,
> Cry—clinging heaven by the hems;
> And lo, Christ walking on the water
> Not of Gennesaret but Thames.

A man may be at his wit's end but he can never be at his hope's end while he has the presence of Christ.

(iv) We are knocked down but not knocked out. The supreme characteristic of the Christian is not that he does not fall, but that every time he falls he rises again. It is not that he is never beaten, but he is never ultimately defeated. He may lose a battle, but he knows that in the end he can never lose the campaign. Browning in his *Epilogue* describes the gallant character:

> One who never turned his back but marched breast forward,
> Never doubted clouds would break,
> Never dreamed, though right were worsted, wrong would triumph,
> Held we fall to rise, are baffled to fight better,
> Sleep to wake.

After he has stated the great paradoxes of the Christian life Paul goes on to give the secret of his own life, the reasons why he was able to do and to endure as he did.

(i) He was well aware that if a man would share the life of Christ he must share his risks, that if a man wished to live with Christ he must be ready to die with him. Paul knew and accepted the inexorable law of the Christian life—"No Cross, No Crown."

(ii) He faced everything in the memory of the power of God who raised Jesus Christ from the dead. He was able to speak with such courage and such disregard of personal safety because he believed that even if death took him, that God could and would also raise him up. He was certain that he could draw on a power which was sufficient for life and greater than death.

(iii) He bore everything in the conviction that through his sufferings and trials others were being led into the light and love of God. The great Boulder Dam scheme in America brought fertility to vast areas which had once been desert. In the making of it there were inevitably those who lost their lives. When the scheme was completed, a tablet was let into the wall of the dam bearing the names of the workmen who had died, and below stands the inscription: "These died that the desert might rejoice and blossom as the rose." Paul could go through what he did because he knew that it was not for nothing; he knew that it was to bring others to Christ. When a man has the conviction that what is happening to him is happening literally for Christ's sake he can face anything.

DAY EIGHTEEN

Citizens of the Kingdom

Philippians 1:27–30

One thing you must see to whatever happens—live a life that is worthy of a citizen of the Kingdom and of the gospel of Christ, so that whether I come and see you, or whether I go away and hear how things go with you, the news will be that you are standing fast, united in one spirit, fighting with one soul the battle of the gospel's faith, and that you are not put into fluttering alarm by any of your adversaries. For your steadfastness is a proof to them that they are doomed to defeat, while you are destined for salvation—and that from God. For to you has been given the privilege of doing something for Christ—the privilege of not only believing in him, but also of suffering for him, for you have the same struggle as that in which you have seen me engaged, and which now you hear that I am undergoing.

One thing is essential—no matter what happens either to them or to Paul the Philippians must live worthily of their faith and profession. Paul chooses his words very carefully. The Authorized Version has it: "Let your conversation be as it becometh the gospel of Christ." Nowadays this is misleading. To us *conversation* means *talk;* but it is derived from the Latin word *conversari,* which means *to conduct oneself.* In the seventeenth century a person's *conversation* was not only his way of speaking to other people; it was his whole behaviour. The phrase means: "Let your behaviour be worthy of those who are pledged to Christ."

But on this occasion Paul uses a word which he very seldom uses in order to express his meaning. The word he would normally use for "to conduct oneself in the ordinary affairs of life" is *peripatein,* which literally means *to walk about;* here he uses *politeuesthai,* which means *to be a citizen.* Paul was writing from the very centre of the Roman Empire, from Rome itself; it was the fact that he was a Roman citizen that had brought him there. Philippi was a Roman colony; and Roman colonies were little bits of Rome planted throughout the world, where the citizens never forgot that they were Romans, spoke the Latin language, wore the Latin dress, called their magistrates by the Latin names, however far they might be from Rome. So what Paul is saying is, "You and I know full well the privileges and the responsibilities of being a Roman citizen. You know full well how even in Philippi, so many miles from Rome, you must still live and act as a Roman does. Well then, remember that you have an even higher duty than that. Wherever you are you must live as befits a citizen of the Kingdom of God.

What does Paul expect from them? He expects them *to stand fast.* The world is full of Christians on the retreat, who, when things grow difficult, play down their Christianity. The true Christian stands fast, unashamed in any company. He expects *unity;* they are to be bound together in one spirit like a band of brothers. Let the world quarrel; Christians must be one. He expects a certain *unconquerability.* Often evil seems invincible; but the Christian must never abandon hope or give up the struggle. He expects a *cool, calm courage.* In times of crisis others may be nervous and afraid; the Christian will be still serene, master of himself and of the situation.

If they can be like that, they will set such an example that the pagans will be disgusted with their own way of life, will realize that the Christians have something they do not possess, and will seek for very self-preservation to share it.

Paul does not suggest that this will be easy. When Christianity first came to Philippi, they saw him fight his own battle. They saw him scourged and imprisoned for the faith (*Acts* 16:19). They know what he is now going through. But let them remember that a general chooses his best soldiers for the hardest tasks, and that it is an honour to suffer for Christ. There is a tale of a veteran French soldier who came in a desperate situation upon a young recruit trembling with fear. "Come, son," said the veteran, "and you and I will do something fine for France." So Paul says to the Philippians: "For you and for me the battle is on; let us do something fine for Christ."

DAY NINETEEN

The Gifts of God

1 Timothy 2:1–7

So then the first thing I urge you to do is to offer your requests, your prayers, your petitions, your thanksgivings for all men. Pray for kings and for all who are in authority, that they may enjoy a life that is tranquil and undisturbed, and that they may act in all godliness and reverence. That is the fine way to live, the way which meets with the approval of God, our Saviour, who wishes all men to be saved, and to come to a full knowledge of the truth. For there is one God, and one Mediator, between God and man, the man Jesus Christ, who gave himself a ransom for all. It was thus he bore his witness to God in his own good times, a witness to which I have been appointed a herald and an envoy (I am speaking the truth: I do not lie), a teacher to the Gentiles, a teacher whose message is based on faith and truth.

The Church prayed for certain things for those in authority.

(i) It prayed for "a life that is tranquil and undisturbed." That was the prayer for freedom from war, from rebellion and from anything which would disturb the peace of the realm. That is the good citizen's prayer for his country.

(ii) But the Church prayed for much more than that. It prayed for "a life that is lived in godliness and reverence." Here we are confronted with two great words which are keynotes of the Pastoral Epistles and describe qualities which not only the ruler but every Christian must covet.

First, there is *godliness, eusebeia.* This is one of the great and almost untranslatable Greek words. It describes reverence both toward God and man. It describes that attitude of mind which respects man and honours God. Eusebius defined it as "reverence towards the one and only God, and the kind of life that he would wish us to lead." To the Greek, the great example of *eusebeia* was Socrates whom Xenophon describes in the following terms: "So pious and devoutly religious that he would take no step apart from the will of heaven; so just and upright that he never did even a trifling injury to any living soul; so self-controlled, so temperate, that he never at any time chose the sweeter in place of the bitter; so sensible and wise and prudent that in distinguishing the better from the worse he never erred" (Xenophon: *Memorabilia,* 4, 8, 11). *Eusebeia* comes very near to that great Latin word *pietas,* which Warde Fowler describes thus: "The quality known to the Romans as *pietas* rises, in spite of trial and danger, superior to the enticements of individual passion and selfish ease. Aeneas's *pietas* became a sense of duty to the will of the gods, as well as to his father, his son and his people; and this duty never leaves him." Clearly *eusebeia* is a tremendous thing. It never forgets the reverence due to God; it never forgets the rights due to men; it never forgets the respect due to self. It describes the character of the man who never fails God, man or himself.

Second, there is reverence, *semnotēs*. Here again we are in the realm of the untranslatable. The corresponding adjective *semnos* is constantly applied to the gods. R. C. Trench says that the man who is *semnos* "has on him a grace and a dignity, not lent by earth." He says that he is one who "without demanding it challenges and inspires reverence." Aristotle was the great ethical teacher of the Greeks. He had a way of describing every virtue as the mean between two extremes. On the one side there was an extreme of excess and on the other an extreme of defect, and in between there was the mean, the happy medium, in which virtue lay. Aristotle says that *semnotēs* is the mean between *areskeia, subservience,* and *authadeia, arrogance.* It may be said that for the man who is *semnos* all life is one act of worship; all life is lived in the presence of God; he moves through the world, as it has been put, as if it was the temple of the living God. He never forgets the holiness of God or the dignity of man.

These two great qualities are regal qualities which every man must covet and for which every man must pray.

Then Paul claims to himself four offices.

(i) He is a *herald* of the story of Jesus Christ. A herald is a man who makes a statement and who says: "This is true." He is a man who brings a proclamation that is not his own, but which comes from the king.

(ii) He is a *witness* to the story of Christ. A witness is a man who says: "This is true, and I know it" and says also "It works." He is a man who tells, not only the story of Christ, but also the story of what Christ has done for him.

(iii) He is an *envoy*. An envoy is one whose duty is to commend his country in a foreign land. An envoy in the Christian sense is therefore one who commends the story of Christ to others. He wishes to communicate that story to others, so that it will mean as much to them as it does to him.

(iv) He is a *teacher*. The *herald* is the person who proclaims the facts; the *witness* is the person who proclaims the power of the facts; the *envoy* is the person who commends the facts; the *teacher* is the person who leads men into the meaning of the facts. It is not enough to know that Christ lived and died; we must think out what that meant. A man must not only feel the wonder of the story of Christ; he must think out its meaning for himself and for the world.

DAY TWENTY

The Nature of Christian Love

1 Corinthians 13:4–7

Love is patient; love is kind; love knows no envy; love is not braggart; it is not inflated with its own importance; it does not behave gracelessly; it does not insist on its rights; it never flies into a temper; it does not store up the memory of any wrong it has received; it finds no pleasure in evildoing; it rejoices with truth; it can endure anything; it is completely trusting; it never ceases to hope; it bears everything with triumphant fortitude."

Paul lists fifteen characteristics of Christian love.

Love is patient. The Greek word (*makrothumein*) used in the New Testament always describes patience with *people* and not patience with circumstances. Chrysostom said that it is the word used of the man who is wronged and who has it easily in his power to avenge himself and who yet will not do it. It describes the man who is slow to anger and it is used of God himself in his relationship with men. In our dealings with men, however refractory and however unkind and hurting they are, we must exercise the same patience as God exercises with us. Such patience is not the sign of weakness but the sign of strength; it is not defeatism but rather the only way to victory. Fosdick points out that no one treated Lincoln with more contempt than did Stanton. He called him "a low cunning clown," he nicknamed him "the original gorilla" and said that Du Chaillu was a fool to wander about Africa trying to capture a gorilla when he could have found one so easily at Springfield, Illinois. Lincoln said nothing. He made

Stanton his war minister because he was the best man for the job and he treated him with every courtesy. The years wore on. The night came when the assassin's bullet murdered Lincoln in the theatre. In the little room to which the President's body was taken stood that same Stanton, and, looking down on Lincoln's silent face, he said through his tears, "There lies the greatest ruler of men the world has ever seen." The patience of love had conquered in the end.

Love is kind. Origen had it that this means that love is "sweet to all." Jerome spoke of what he called "the benignity" of love. So much Christianity is good but unkind. There was no more religious a man than Philip the Second of Spain, and yet he founded the Spanish Inquisition and thought he was serving God by massacring those who thought differently from him. The famous Cardinal Pole declared that murder and adultery could not compare in heinousness with heresy. Apart altogether from that persecuting spirit, there is in so many good people an attitude of criticism. So many good Church people would have sided with the rulers and not with Jesus if they had had to deal with the woman taken in adultery.

Love knows no envy. It has been said that there are really only two classes of people in this world—"those who are millionaires and those who would like to be." There are two kinds of envy. The one covets the possessions of other people; and such envy is very difficult to avoid because it is a very human thing. The other is worse—it grudges the very fact that others should have what it has not; it does not so much want things for itself as wish that others had not got them. Meanness of soul can sink no further than that.

Love is no braggart. There is a self-effacing quality in love. True love will always be far more impressed with its own unworthiness than its own merit. In Barrie's story Sentimental Tommy used to come home to his mother after some success at school and say, "Mother, am I no' a wonder?" Some people confer their love with the idea that they are conferring a favour. But the real lover cannot ever get over the wonder that he is loved. Love is kept humble by the consciousness that it can never offer its loved one a gift which is good enough.

Love is not inflated with its own importance. Napoleon always advocated the sanctity of the home and the obligation of public worship—for others. Of himself he said, "I am not a man like other men. The laws of morality do not apply to me." The really great man never thinks of his own importance. Carey, who began life as a cobbler, was one of the greatest missionaries and certainly one of the greatest linguists the world has ever seen. He translated at least parts of the Bible into no fewer than thirty-four Indian languages. When he came to India, he was regarded with dislike and contempt. At a dinner party a snob, with the idea of humiliating him, said in a tone that everyone could hear, "I suppose, Mr. Carey, you once worked as a shoe-maker." "No, your lordship," answered Carey, "not a shoe-maker, only a cobbler." He did not even claim to make shoes—only to mend them. No one likes the "important" person. Man "dressed in a little brief authority" can be a sorry sight.

Love does not behave gracelessly. It is a significant fact that in Greek the words for *grace* and for *charm* are the same. There is a kind of Christianity which takes a delight in being blunt and almost brutal. There is strength in it but there is no winsomeness. Lightfoot of Durham said of Arthur F. Sim, one of his students, "Let him go where he will, his face will be a sermon in itself." There is a graciousness in Christian love which never forgets that courtesy and tact and politeness are lovely things.

Love does not insist upon its rights. In the last analysis, there are in this world only two kinds of people—those who always insist upon their privileges and those who always remember their responsibilities; those who are always thinking of what life owes them and those who never forget what they owe to life. It would be the key to almost all the problems which surround us today if men would think less of their rights and more of their duties. Whenever we start thinking about "our place," we are drifting away from Christian love.

Love never flies into a temper. The real meaning of this is that Christian love never becomes exasperated with people. Exasperation is always a sign of defeat. When we lose our tempers, we lose everything. Kipling said that it was the test of a man if he could keep his head when everyone else was losing his and blaming it on him, and if when he was hated he did not give way to hating. The man who is master of his temper can be master of anything.

Love does not store up the memory of any wrong it has received. The word translated *store up* (*logizeshthai*) is an accountant's word. It is the word used for entering up an item in a ledger so that it will not be forgotten. That is precisely what so many people do. One of the great arts in life is to learn what to forget. A writer tells how "in Polynesia, where the natives spend much of their time in fighting and feasting, it is customary for each man to keep some reminders of his hatred. Articles are suspended from the roofs of their huts to keep alive the memory of their wrongs—real or imaginary." In the same way many people nurse their wrath to keep it warm; they brood over their wrongs until it is impossible to forget them. Christian love has learned the great lesson of forgetting.

Love finds no pleasure in evil-doing. It might be better to translate this that love finds no pleasure in anything that is wrong. It is not so much delight in doing the wrong thing that is meant, as the malicious pleasure which comes to most of us when we hear something derogatory about someone else. It is one of the queer traits of human nature that very often we prefer to hear of the misfortune of others rather than of their good fortune. It is much easier to weep with them that weep than to rejoice with those who rejoice. Christian love has none of that human malice which finds pleasure in all reports.

Love rejoices with the truth. That is not so easy as it sounds. There are times when we definitely do not want the truth to prevail; and still more times when it is the last thing we wish to hear. Christian love has no wish to veil the truth; it has nothing to conceal and so is glad when the truth prevails.

Love can endure anything. It is just possible that this may mean "love can cover anything," in the sense that it will never drag into the light of day the faults and mistakes of others. It would far rather set about quietly mending things than publicly displaying and rebuking them. More likely it means that love can bear any insult, any injury, any disappointment. It describes the kind of love that was in the heart of Jesus himself:

Thy foes might hate, despise, revile,
Thy friends unfaithful prove;
Unwearied in forgiveness still,
Thy heart could only love.

Love is completely trusting. This characteristic has a twofold aspect. (i) *In relation to God* it means that love takes God at his word, and can take every promise which begins "Whosoever" and say, "That means me." (ii) *In relation to our fellow-men* it means that love always believes the best about other people. It is often true that we make people what we believe them to be. If we show that we do not trust people, we may make them untrustworthy. If we show people that we trust them absolutely, we may make them trustworthy. When Arnold became headmaster of Rugby he instituted a completely new way of doing things. Before him, school had been a terror and a tyranny. Arnold called the boys together and told them that there was going to be much more liberty and much less flogging. "You are free," he said, "but you are responsible—you are gentlemen. I intend to leave you much to yourselves, and put you upon your honour, because I believe that if you are guarded and watched and spied upon, you will grow up knowing only the fruits of servile fear; and when your liberty is finally given you, as it must be some day, you will not know how to use it." The boys found it difficult to believe. When they were brought before him they continued to make the old excuses and to tell the old lies. "Boys," he said, "if you say so, it must be true—I believe your word." The result was that there came a time in Rugby when boys said, "It is a shame to tell Arnold a lie—he always believes you." He believed in them and he made them what he believed them to be. Love can ennoble even the ignoble by believing the best.

Love never ceases to hope. Jesus believed that no man is hopeless. Adam Clark was one of the great theologians but at school he was very slow to learn. One day a distinguished visitor paid a visit to the school, and the teacher singled out Adam Clark and said, "That is the stupidest boy in the school." Before he left the school, the visitor came to the boy and said kindly, "Never mind, my boy, you may be a great scholar some day. Don't be discouraged but try hard, and keep on trying." The teacher was hopeless, the visitor was hopeful, and—who knows?—it may well have been that word of hope which made Adam Clark what he one day became.

Love bears everything with triumphant fortitude. The verb used here (*hupomenein*) is one of the great Greek words. It is generally translated *to bear* or *to endure;* but what it really describes is not the spirit which can passively bear things, but the spirit which, in bearing them, can conquer and transmute them. It has been defined as "a masculine constancy under trial." George Matheson, who lost his sight and who was disappointed in love, wrote in one of his prayers that he might accept God's will, "Not with dumb resignation but with holy joy; not only with the absence of murmur but with a song of praise." Love can bear things, not merely with passive resignation, but with triumphant fortitude, because it knows that "a father's hand will never cause his child a needless tear."

One thing remains to be said—when we think of the qualities of this love as Paul portrays them we can see them realized in the life of Jesus himself.

DAY TWENTY-ONE

How Much Do You Want Goodness?

Mark 10:17–22

As Jesus was going along the road, a man came running to him and threw himself at his feet and asked him, "Good teacher, what am I to do to inherit eternal life?" Jesus said to him, "Why do you call me good? There is no one who is good, except one—God. You know the commandments. You must not kill, you must not commit adultery, you must not steal, you must not bear false witness, you must not defraud anyone, you must honour your father and mother." He said to him, "Teacher, I have kept all these from my youth." When Jesus looked at him he loved him, and he said to him. "You still lack one thing. Go, sell all that you have, and give it to the poor and you will have treasure in heaven. And come! Follow me!" But he was grieved at this saying, and he went away in sadness, for he had many possessions.

Here is one of the most vivid stories in the gospels.

(i) We must note how the man came and how Jesus met him. He came running. He flung himself at Jesus' feet. There is something amazing in the sight of this rich, young aristocrat falling at the feet of the penniless prophet from Nazareth, who was on the way to being an outlaw. "Good teacher!" he began. And straight away Jesus answered back, "No flattery! Don't call me good! Keep that word for God!" It looks almost as if Jesus was trying to freeze him and to pour cold water on that young enthusiasm.

There is a lesson here. It is clear that this man came to Jesus in a moment of overflowing emotion. It is also clear that Jesus exercised a personal fascination over him. Jesus did two things that every evangelist and every preacher and every teacher ought to remember and to copy.

First, he said in effect, "Stop and think! You are all wrought up and palpitating with emotion! I don't want you swept to me by a moment of emotion. Think calmly what you are doing." Jesus was not freezing the man. He was telling him even at the very outset to count the cost.

Second, he said in effect, "You cannot become a Christian by a sentimental passion for me. *You must look at God.*" Preaching and teaching always mean the conveying of truth through personality, and thereby lies the greatest danger of the greatest teachers. The danger is that the pupil, the scholar, the young person may form a personal attachment to the teacher or the preacher and think that it is an attachment to God. The teacher and preacher must never point to himself. He must always point to God. There is in all true teaching a certain self-obliteration. True, we cannot keep personality and warm personal loyalty out of it altogether, and we would not if we could. But the matter must not stop there. The teacher and the preacher are in the last analysis only finger-posts to God.

(ii) Never did any story so lay down the essential Christian truth that *respectability is not enough.* Jesus quoted the commandments which were the basis of the decent life. Without hesitation the man said he had kept them all. Note one thing—with one exception they were all negative commandments, and that one exception operated only in the family circle. In effect the man was saying, "I never in my life did any-one any harm." That was perfectly true. But the real question is, "What good have you done?" And the question to this man was even more pointed, "With all your possessions, with your wealth, with all that you could give away, what positive good have you done to others? How much have you gone out of your way to help and comfort and strengthen others as you might have done?" Respectability, on the whole, consists in *not doing things;* Christianity consists in *doing things.* That was precisely where this man—like so many of us—fell down.

(iii) So Jesus confronted him with a challenge. In effect he said, "Get out of this moral respectability. Stop looking at goodness as con-sisting in not doing things. Take yourself and all that you have, and spend everything on others. Then you will find true happiness in time and in eternity." The man could not do it. He had great possessions, which it had never entered his head to give away and when it was sug-gested to him he could not. True, he had never stolen, and he had never defrauded anyone—but neither had he ever been, nor could he compel himself to be, positively and sacrificially generous.

It may be respectable never to take away from anyone. It is Chris-tian to give to someone. In reality Jesus was confronting this man with a basic and essential question—"How much do you want real Chris-tianity? Do you want it enough to give your possessions away?" And the man had to answer in effect, "I want it—but I don't want it as much as all that."

Robert Louis Stevenson in *The Master of Ballantrae* draws a pic-ture of the master leaving the ancestral home of Durrisdeer for the last time. Even he is sad. He is talking to the faithful family steward. "Ah! M'Kellar," he said, "do you think I have never a regret?" "I do not think," said M'Kellar, "that you could be so bad a man unless you had all the machinery for being a good one." "Not all," said the master, "not all. It is there you are in error. The malady of not wanting."

It was the malady of not wanting enough which meant tragedy for the man who came running to Jesus. It is the malady from which most of us suffer. We all want goodness, but so few of us want it enough to pay the price.

Jesus, looking at him, loved him. There were many things in that look of Jesus.

(*a*) There was the appeal of love. Jesus was not angry with him. He loved him too much for that. It was not the look of anger but the appeal of love.

(*b*) There was the challenge to chivalry. It was a look which sought to pull the man out of his comfortable, respectable, settled life into the adventure of being a real Christian.

(*c*) It was the look of grief. And that grief was the sorest grief of all—the grief of seeing a man deliberately choose not to be what he might have been and had it in him to be.

Jesus looks at us with the appeal of love and with the challenge to the knightliness of the Christian way. God grant that he may never have to look at us with sorrow for a loved one who refuses to be what he might have been and could have been.

DAY TWENTY-TWO

The Unwritten Law

Romans 2:12–16

As many as sinned without the law shall also perish without the law; and as many as sinned in the law shall be judged by the law; for it is not the hearers of the law who are righteous in the sight of God, but it is the doers of the law who will be accounted righteous, in that day when God judges the hidden things of men according to my gospel through Jesus Christ. For whenever the Gentiles, who do not possess the law, do by nature the deeds of the law, they, although they do not possess the law, are a law to themselves. They show the work of the law written on their hearts, while their consciences bear them witness, and while their thoughts within accuse or excuse them.

In the translation we have slightly changed the order of the verses. In the sense of the passage verse 16 follows verse 13, and verses 14 and 15 are a long parenthesis. It is to be remembered that Paul was not writing this letter sitting at a desk and thinking out every word and every construction. He was striding up and down the room dictating it to his secretary, Tertius (*Romans* 16:22), who struggled to get it down. That explains the long parenthesis, but it is easier to get the correct meaning in English if we go straight from verse 13 to verse 16, and add verses 14 and 15 afterward.

In this passage Paul turns to the Gentiles. He has dealt with the Jews and with their claims to special privilege. But one advantage the Jew did have, and that was the Law. A Gentile might well retaliate by saying, "It is only right that God should condemn the Jews, who had the Law and who ought to have known better; but we will surely escape judgment because we had no opportunity to know the Law and did not know any better." In answer Paul lays down two great principles.

(i) A man will be judged by what he had the opportunity to know. If he knew the Law, he will be judged as one who knew the Law. If he did not know the Law, he will be judged as one who did not know the Law. God is fair. And here is the answer to those who ask what is to happen to the people who lived in the world before Jesus came and who had no opportunity to hear the Christian message. A man will be judged by his fidelity to the highest that it was possible for him to know.

(ii) Paul goes on to say that even those who did not know the written Law had an unwritten law within their hearts. We would call it the instinctive knowledge of right and wrong. The Stoics said that in the universe there were certain laws operative which a man broke at his peril—the laws of health, the moral laws which govern life and living. The Stoics called these laws *phusis*, which means *nature*, and urged men to live *kata phusin*, according to nature. It is Paul's argument that in the very nature of man there is an instinctive knowledge of what he ought to do. The Greeks would have agreed with that. Aristotle said: "The cultivated and free-minded man will so behave as being *a law to himself.*" Plutarch asks: "Who shall govern the governor?" And he answers: "Law, the king of all mortals and immortals, as Pindar calls it, which is not written on papyrus rolls or wooden tablets, but is his own reason within the soul, which perpetually dwells with him and guards him and never leaves his soul bereft of leadership."

Paul saw the world divided into two classes of people. He saw the

Jews with their Law given to them direct from God and written down so that all could read it. He saw the other nations, without this written law, but nonetheless with a God-implanted knowledge of right and wrong within their hearts. Neither could claim exemption from the judgment of God. The Jew could not claim exemption on the ground that he had a special place in God's plan. The Gentile could not claim exemption on the ground that he had never received the written Law. The Jew would be judged as one who had known the Law; the Gentile as one who had a God-given conscience. God will judge a man according to what he knows and has the chance to know.

DAY TWENTY-THREE

Respect for the Weaker Brother

Romans 14:21–23

It is the fine thing neither to eat meat, nor to drink wine, nor to do anything which makes the road more difficult for your brother to walk. As far as you yourselves are concerned you have enough faith to know that these things do not matter—well, then, let that be a matter between yourself and God. Happy is the man who never has cause to condemn himself for doing what he has come to the conclusion it was right to do. But he who has doubts about eating something stands condemned if he does eat it, because his decision to eat is not the result of faith.

We are back at the point that what is right for one man may be the ruin of another. Paul's advice is very practical.

(i) He has advice for the man who is strong in the faith. That man knows that food and drink make no difference. He has grasped the principle of Christian freedom. Well, then, let that freedom be something between him and God. He has reached this stage of faith; and God knows well that he has reached it. But that is no reason why he should flaunt his freedom in the face of the man who has not yet reached it. Many a man has insisted on the rights of his freedom, and then had cause to regret that he ever did so when he sees the consequences.

A man may come to the conclusion that his Christian freedom gives him a perfect right to make a reasonable use of alcohol; and, as far as he is concerned, it may be a perfectly safe pleasure, from which he runs no danger. But it may be that a younger man who admires him is watching him and taking him as an example. And it may also be that this younger man is one of these people to whom alcohol is a fatal thing. Is the older man to use his Christian freedom to go on setting an example which may well be the ruin of his young admirer? Or is he to limit himself, not for his own sake, but for the sake of the one who follows in his footsteps?

Surely conscious limitation for the sake of others is the Christian thing. If a man does not exercise it, he may well find that something that he genuinely thought to be permissible has brought ruin to someone else! It is surely better to make this deliberate limitation than to have the remorse of knowing that what one demanded as a pleasure has become death to someone else. Again and again, in every sphere of life, the Christian is confronted with the fact that he must examine things, not only as they affect himself, but also as they affect other people. A man is always in some sense his brother's keeper, responsible, not only for himself, but for everyone who comes into contact with him. "His friendship did me a mischief," said Burns of the older man he met in Irvine as he learned the art of flax-dressing. God grant that none may say that of us because we misused the glory of Christian freedom!

(ii) Paul has advice for the man who is weak in the faith, the man with the over-scrupulous conscience. This man may disobey or silence his scruples. He may sometimes do something because everyone else is doing it and he does not wish to be different. He may do it because he does not wish to court ridicule or unpopularity. Paul's answer is that if a man defies his conscience he is guilty of sin. If a man believes a thing to be wrong, then, if he does it, for him it is sin. A neutral thing becomes a right thing only when it is done out of the real, reasoned conviction that it is right. No man is the keeper of another man's conscience, and each man's conscience, in things indifferent, must be the arbiter for him of what is right or wrong.

DAY TWENTY-FOUR

The Christian's Duty

2 Timothy 4:1–5

I charge you before God and Christ Jesus, who is going to judge the living and the dead—I charge you by his appearing and by his Kingdom—herald forth the word; be urgent in season and out of season; convict, rebuke, exhort, and do it all with a patience and a teaching which never fail. For there will come a time when men will refuse to listen to sound teaching, but, because they have ears which have to be continually titillated with novelties, they will bury themselves under a mound of teachers, whose teaching suits their own lusts after forbidden things. They will avert their ears from the truth, and they will turn to extravagant tales. As for you, be steady in all things; accept the suffering which will come upon you; do the work of an evangelist; leave no act of your service unfulfilled.

There can be few New Testament passages where the duties of the Christian teacher are more clearly set out than here.

The Christian teacher is to be *urgent*. The message he brings is literally a matter of life and death. The teachers who really get their message across are those who have the note of earnestness in their voice. Spurgeon had a real admiration for Martineau, who was a Unitarian and therefore denied the divinity of Jesus Christ which Spurgeon believed in with passionate intensity. Someone once said to Spurgeon: "How can you possibly admire Martineau? You don't believe what he preaches." "No," said Spurgeon, "*but he does.*" Any man with the note of urgency in his voice demands, and will receive, a hearing from other men.

The Christian teacher is to be *persistent*. He is to urge the claims of Christ "in season and out of season." As someone has put it: "Take or make your opportunity." As Theodore of Mospeuestia put it: "The Christian must count every time an opportunity to speak for Christ." It was said of George Morrison of Wellington Church in Glasgow that with him wherever the conversation started, it went straight across country to Christ. This does not mean that we will not choose our time to speak, for there should be courtesy in evangelism as in every other human contact; but it does mean that perhaps we are far too shy in speaking to others about Jesus Christ.

Paul goes on to speak of the effect the Christian witness must produce.

He must *convict*. He must make the sinner aware of his sin. Walter Bagehot once said: "The road to perfection lies through a series of disgusts." Somehow or other the sinner must be made to feel disgusted with his sin. Epictetus draws a contrast between the false philosopher, who is out for popularity, and the real philosopher, whose one aim is the good of his hearers. The false philosopher deals in flattery and panders to self-esteem. The real philosopher says: "Come and be told that you are in a bad way." "The philosopher's lecture," he said, "is a surgery; when you go away you ought to have felt not pleasure, but pain." It was Alcibiades, the brilliant but spoiled darling of Athens, who used to say to Socrates: "Socrates, I hate you, because every time I meet you, you make me see what I am." The first essential is to compel a man to see himself as he is.

He must *rebuke*. In the great days of the Church there was an utter fearlessness in its voice; and because of that things happened. Ambrose of Milan was one of the great figures of the early Church. He was an intimate friend of Theodosius, the Emperor, who was a Christian, but a man of violent temper. Ambrose never hesitated to tell the Emperor the truth. "Who," he demanded, "will dare to tell you the truth if a priest does not dare?" Theodosius had appointed one of his close friends, Botherich, as governor of Thessalonica. Botherich, a good governor, had occasion to imprison a famous charioteer for infamous conduct. The popularity of these charioteers was incredible and the populace rose in a riot and murdered Botherich. Theodosius was mad with anger. Ambrose pled with him for discrimination in punishment, but Rufinus, his minister of state, deliberately inflamed his anger and Theodosius sent out orders for a massacre of vengeance. Later he countermanded the order, but too late for the new order to reach Thessalonica in time. The theatre was crammed to capacity with the doors shut, and the soldiers of Theodosius went to and fro slaughtering men, women and children for three hours. More than seven thousand people were killed. News of the massacre came back to Milan and when Theodosius presented himself at the Church service the next Sunday, Ambrose refused him admission. The Emperor pled for pardon. Eight months passed and again he came to Church. Again Ambrose refused him entry. In the end the Emperor of Rome had to lie prostrate on the ground with the penitents before he was allowed to worship with the Church again. In its great days the Church was fearless in rebuke.

In our personal relationships a word of warning and rebuke would often save a brother from sin and shipwreck. But, as someone has said, that word must always be spoken as "brother setting brother right." It must be spoken with a consciousness of our common guilt. It is not our place to set ourselves up as moral judges of anyone; nonetheless it is our duty to speak that warning word when it needs to be spoken.

He must *exhort.* Here is the other side of the matter. No rebuke should ever be such that it drives a man to despair and takes the heart and the hope out of him. Not only must men be rebuked, they must also be encouraged.

Further, the Christian duty of conviction, of rebuke and of encouragement must be carried out with unwearied *patience.* The word is *makrothumia,* and it describes the spirit which never grows irritated, never despairs and never regards any man as beyond salvation. The Christian patiently believes in men because he unconquerably believes in the changing power of Christ.

DAY TWENTY-FIVE

God's Fidelity and Man's Infidelity

Romans 3:1–8

What, then, is the something plus which belongs to a Jew? Or what special advantage belongs to those who have been circumcised? Much in every way. In the first place, there is this advantage—that the Jews have been entrusted with the oracles of God. Yes, you say, but what if some of them were unfaithful to them? Surely you are not going to argue that their infidelity invalidates the fidelity of God? God forbid! Let God be shown to be true, though every man be shown to be a liar, as it stands written: "In order that you may be seen to be in the right in your arguments, and that you may win your case when you enter into judgment." But, you say, if our unrighteousness merely provides proof of God's righteousness, what are we to say? Surely you are not going to try to argue that God is unrighteous to unleash the Wrath upon you? (I am using human arguments:) God forbid! For, if that were so, how shall God judge the world? But, you say, if the fact that I am false merely provides a further opportunity to demonstrate the fact that God is true, to his greater glory, why should I still be condemned as a sinner? Are you going to argue—just as some slanderously allege that we suggest—that we should do evil that good may come of it? Anyone can see that statements like that merit nothing but condemnation.

Here Paul is arguing in the closest and the most difficult way. It will make it easier to understand if we remember that he is carrying on an argument with an imaginary objector. The argument stated in full would run something like this.

The objector: The result of all that you have been saying is that there is no difference between Gentile and Jew and that they are in exactly the same position. Do you really mean that?

Paul: By no means.

The objector: What, then, is the difference?

Paul: For one thing, the Jew possesses what the Gentile never so directly possessed—the commandments of God.

The objector: Granted! But what if some of the Jews disobeyed these commandments and were unfaithful to God and came under his condemnation? You have just said that God gave the Jews a special position and a special promise. Now you go on to say that at least some of them are under the condemnation of God. Does that mean that God has broken his promise and shown himself to be unjust and unreliable?

Paul: Far from it! What it does show is that there is no favouritism with God and that he punishes sin wherever he sees it. The very fact that he condemns the unfaithful Jews is the best possible proof of his absolute justice. He might have been expected to overlook the sins of this special people of his but he does not.

The objector: Very well then! All you have done is to succeed in showing that my disobedience has given God an opportunity to demonstrate his righteousness. My infidelity has given God a marvellous opportunity to demonstrate his fidelity. My sin is, therefore, an excellent thing! It has given God a chance to show how good he is! I may have done evil, but good has come of it! You can't surely condemn a man for giving God a chance to show his justice!

Paul: An argument like that is beneath contempt! You have only to state it to see how intolerable it is!

When we disentangle this passage in this way, we see that there are in it certain basic thoughts of Paul in regard to the Jews.

(i) To the end of the day he believed the Jews to be in a special position in regard to God. That, in fact, is what they believed themselves. The difference was that Paul believed that their special position was one of special *responsibility;* the Jew believed it to be one of special *privilege.* What did Paul say that the Jew had been specially entrusted with? *The oracles of God.* What does he mean by that? The word he uses is *logia,* the regular word in the Greek Old Testament for a special statement or pronouncement of God. Here it means *The Ten Commandments.* God entrusted the Jews with *commandments,* not privileges. He said to them, "You are a special people; therefore you must live a special life." He did *not* say, "You are a special people; therefore you can do what you like." He did say, "You are a special people; *therefore you must do what I like.*" When Lord Dunsany came in safety through the 1914–18 war he tells us that he said to himself, "In some strange way I am still alive. I wonder what God means me to do with a life so specially spared?" That thought never struck the Jews. They never could grasp the fact that God's special choice was for special duty.

(ii) All through his writings there are three basic facts in Paul's mind about the Jews. They occur in embryo here; and they are in fact the three thoughts that it takes this whole letter to work out. We must note that he does not place all the Jews under the one condemnation. He puts it in this way: "What if *some of them* were unfaithful?"

(*a*) He was quite sure that God was justified in condemning the Jews. They had their special place and their special promises; and that very fact made their condemnation all the greater. Responsibility is always the obverse of privilege. The more opportunity a man has to do right, the greater his condemnation if he does wrong.

(*b*) *But* not all of them were unfaithful. Paul never forgot the faithful remnant; and he was quite sure that that faithful remnant—however small it was in numbers—was the true Jewish race. The others had lost their privileges and were under condemnation. They were no longer Jews at all. The remnant was the real nation.

(*c*) Paul was always sure that God's rejection of Israel *was not final.* Because of this rejection, a door was opened to the Gentiles; and, *in the end,* the Gentiles would bring the Jews back within the fold, and Gentile and Jew would be one in Christ. The tragedy of the Jew was that the great task of world evangelization that he might have had, and was designed to have, was refused by him. It was therefore given to the Gentiles, and God's plan was, as it were, reversed, and it was not, as it should have been, the Jew who evangelized the Gentile, but the Gentile who evangelized the Jew—a process which is still going on.

Further, this passage contains two great universal human truths.

(i) The root of all sin is disobedience. The root of the Jew's sin was disobedience to the known law of God. As Milton wrote, it was "man's first disobedience" which was responsible for paradise lost. When pride sets up the will of man against the will of God, there is sin. If there were no disobedience, there would be no sin.

(ii) Once a man has sinned, he displays an amazing ingenuity in justifying his sin. Here we come across an argument that reappears again and again in religious thought, the argument that sin gives God a chance to show at once his justice and his mercy and is therefore a good thing. It is a twisted argument. One might as well argue—it would, in fact, be the same argument—that it is a good thing to break a person's heart, because it gives him a chance to show how much he loves you. When a man sins, the need is not for ingenuity to justify his sin, but for humility to confess it in penitence and in shame.

DAY TWENTY-SIX

The Marks of the Fellowship

Romans 15:1–6

It is the duty of us who are strong to bear the weaknesses of those who are not strong, and not to please ourselves. Let each one of us please our neighbour, but always for his good and always for his upbuilding in the faith. For the Anointed One of God did not please himself, but, as it stands written, "The insults of those who were insulting you fell upon me." All the things that were written long ago were written to teach us, so that, through our fortitude, and through the encouragement which the scriptures give, we may hold fast to our hope. May the God who inspires us with fortitude, and gives us encouragement, grant to you to live in harmony with one another as Christ Jesus would have you to do, so that your praise to the God and Father of our Lord Jesus Christ may rise from a united heart and a united voice.

Paul is still dealing with the duties of those within the Christian fellowship to one another, and especially with the duty of the stronger to the weaker brother. This passage gives us a wonderful summary of the marks which should characterize that fellowship.

(i) The Christian fellowship should be marked by the *consideration* of its members for each other. Always their thoughts should be, not for themselves, but for each other. But this consideration must not degenerate into an easy-going, sentimental laxity. It must always be designed for the other person's good and for his upbuilding in the faith. It is not the toleration which tolerates because it is too lazy to do anything else. It is the toleration which knows that a man may be won much more easily to a fuller faith by surrounding him with an atmosphere of love than by attacking him with a battery of criticism.

(ii) The Christian fellowship should be marked by the *study of scripture;* and from that study of scripture the Christian draws *encouragement.* Scripture, from this point of view, provides us with two things. (*a*) It gives us the record of God's dealing with a nation, a record which is the demonstration that it is always better to be right with God and to suffer, than to be wrong with men and to avoid trouble. The history of Israel is the demonstration in the events of history that ultimately it is well with good and evil with the wicked. Scripture demonstrates, not that God's way is ever an easy way, but in the end it is the only way to everything that makes life worthwhile in time and in eternity. (*b*) It gives us the great and precious promises of God. It is said that Alexander Whyte sometimes had a habit of uttering one text when he left some home during his pastoral visitation; and, as he uttered it, he would say: "Put that under your tongue and suck it like a sweetie." These promises are the promises of a God who never breaks his word. In these ways scripture gives to the man who studies it comfort in his sorrow and encouragement in his struggle.

(iii) The Christian fellowship should be marked by *fortitude.* Fortitude is an attitude of the heart to life. Again we meet this great word *hupomonē*. It is far more than patience; it is the triumphant adequacy which can cope with life; it is the strength which does not only accept things, but which, in accepting them, transmutes them into glory.

(iv) The Christian fellowship should be marked by *hope.* The Christian is always a realist, but never a pessimist. The Christian hope is not a cheap hope. It is not the immature hope which is optimistic because it does not see the difficulties and has not encountered the experiences of life. It might be thought that hope is the prerogative of the young; but the great artists did not think that. When Watts drew "Hope" he drew her as a battered and bowed figure with one string left upon her lyre. The Christian hope has seen everything and endured everything, and still has not despaired, because it believes in God. It is not hope in the human spirit, in human goodness, in human achievement; it is hope in the power of God.

(v) The Christian fellowship should be marked by *harmony.* However ornate a church may be, however perfect its worship and its music, however liberal its giving, it has lost the very first essential of a Christian fellowship if it has lost harmony. That is not to say that there will not be differences of opinion; it is not to say that there will be no argument and debate; but it means that those who are within the Christian fellowship will have solved the problem of living together. They will be quite sure that the Christ who unites them is greater by far than the differences which may divide them.

(vi) The Christian fellowship should be marked by *praise*. It is not a bad test of a man to ask whether the main accent of his voice is that of grumbling discontent or cheerful thanksgiving. "What can I do, who am a little old lame man," said Epictetus, "except give praise to God?" The Christian should enjoy life because he enjoys God. He will carry his secret within him, for he will be sure that God is working all things together for good.

(vii) And the essence of the matter is that the Christian fellowship takes its example, its inspiration and its dynamic from Jesus Christ. He did not please himself. The quotation which Paul uses is from *Psalm* 69:9. It is significant that when Paul speaks of *bearing* the weaknesses of others he uses the same word as is used of Christ bearing his Cross (*bastazein*). When the Lord of Glory chose to serve others instead of to please himself, he set the pattern which every one who seeks to be his follower must accept.

DAY TWENTY-SEVEN

The False and the True Worship

1 Corinthians 14:1–19

Pursue this love. Covet the spiritual things, especially the gift of forthtelling the truth to others. For he who speaks in a tongue does not speak to men but to God, for no one can understand. By the Spirit he speaks things which only the initiated can understand. But he who forthtells the truth to men speaks something which builds them up and encourages them and comforts them. He who speaks in a tongue builds up his own spiritual life, but he who forthtells the truth builds up the spiritual life of the Church. I wish that you could all speak with tongues, but I wish still more that you could all forthtell the truth. He who forthtells the truth is greater than he who speaks with tongues, unless the tongues are interpreted so that the

Church may receive spiritual upbuilding. Now, brothers, if I come to you speaking with tongues what good would I do you? I cannot do you any good unless I speak to you through some special message given to me direct by God, or with some special knowledge, or with the forthtelling of the truth, or with teaching. There are instruments which, though they are lifeless, have a voice—for example, the flute and the harp—but if they do not observe the correct intervals between the notes, how can the tune that is being played on the flute or the harp be recognized? If the trumpet gives a meaningless sound, who will prepare for the battle? So, too, if you produce in a tongue speech the meaning of which cannot be grasped, how can what is being said be understood? You might as well be talking to the air. There are so many voices—whatever the number of them may be—in the world and nothing is without a voice. So then if I do not understand what the voice is trying to say, I will be a foreigner to him who speaks and he who speaks will be a foreigner as far as I am concerned. So, when you are eager for spiritual gifts, be eager to excel in gifts which are useful for the upbuilding of the Church. Therefore let him who speaks in a tongue pray to be able to interpret what he says, for, if I pray in a tongue, my spirit prays, but my mind gets no benefit at all. What then emerges from all this? I will pray with the spirit, but I will pray with my mind too. I will sing with the spirit, but I will sing with my mind too. For if you are blessing God in the spirit, how can the man who occupies the position of a simple layman say the customary Amen to your thanksgiving, since he does not understand what you are saying? It is a fine thing that you give thanks, but the other man receives no spiritual upbuilding. I thank God that I can speak with tongues more than any of you. But in any Christian gathering I would rather speak five words with my intelligence, so that I may teach others as well, rather than ten thousand words in a tongue.

This chapter is very difficult to understand because it deals with a phenomenon which, for most of us, is outside our experience. Throughout Paul sets two spiritual gifts in comparison with each other.

First there is *speaking with tongues*. This phenomenon was very common in the early Church. A man became worked up to an ecstasy and in that state poured out a quite uncontrollable torrent of sounds in no known language. Unless these sounds were interpreted, no one had any idea what they meant. Strange as it may seem to many of us, in the early Church this was a highly coveted gift. It was dangerous. For one thing, it was abnormal and was greatly admired and therefore the person who possessed it was very liable to develop a certain spiritual pride; and for another thing, the very desire to possess it produced, at least in some, a kind of self-hypnotism and deliberately induced hysteria which issued in a completely false and synthetic speaking with tongue.

Over against this speaking with tongues, Paul sets the gift of *prophecy*. In the translation we have not used the word *prophecy,* for that would have further complicated an already complicated situation. In this case, and in fact usually, it has nothing to do with foretelling the future but everything to do with forthtelling the will and the message of God. We have already said that preaching very nearly gives the meaning, but in this case we have kept the literal meaning and have translated it *forthtelling*.

In this whole section Paul deals with the dangers of the gift of speaking with tongues, and the superiority of the gift of forthtelling the truth in such a way that all can understand it.

Out of this difficult section emerge certain valuable truths.

Verse 3 succinctly lays down the aim of all preaching. It is threefold. (i) It must aim *to build up;* to increase a man's knowledge of Christian truth and his ability to live the Christian life. (ii) It must aim *to encourage.* In every group of people there are those who are depressed and discouraged. Dreams will not come true; effort seems to have achieved so little; self-examination serves to show nothing but failures and inadequacies. Within the Christian fellowship, a man should find something to cheer his heart and nerve his arm. It was said of a certain preacher that he preached the gospel as if he were announcing a deep depression off Iceland. A service may begin by humbling a man through showing him his sin, but it is a failure unless it ends by pointing him to the grace of God that can enable him to conquer it. (iii) It must aim *to comfort.* "Never morning wore to evening but some heart did break." There are what Virgil called, "the tears of things." In any company of people there will always be some whom life has hurt; and within the Christian fellowship they must be able to find beauty for their ashes, the oil of joy for mourning and the garment of praise for the spirit of their heaviness.

Verse 5 gives us the things which for Paul were the background and the substance of all preaching. (i) It comes from *a direct revelation from God.* No man can speak to others unless God has first spoken to him. It was said of a great preacher that ever and again he paused as if listening for a voice. We never give to men or to scholars truth which we have produced, or even discovered; we transmit truth which has been given to us. (ii) It may bring *some special knowledge.* No man can possibly be an expert in everything, but every man has special knowledge of something. It has been said that any man can write an interesting book if he will simply set down completely honestly all that has happened to him. The experiences of life give something special to each one of us, and the most effective preaching is simply witness to what we have found to be true. (iii) It consists of *forthtelling the truth.* In the early Church the first preaching given to any fellowship was a simple proclamation of the facts of the Christian story. Certain things are beyond argument. "Tell me of your certainties," said Goethe, "I have doubts enough of my own." However we may finish, it is well to begin with the facts of Christ. (iv) It goes on to *teaching.* There comes a time when a man has to ask, "What is the meaning of these facts?" Simply because we are thinking creatures, religion implies theology. And it may well be that the faith of many people collapses and the loyalty of many people grows cold because they have not thought things out and thought them through.

From the whole passage two broad principles regarding Christian worship emerge.

(i) *Worship must never be selfish.* All that is done in it must be done for the sake of all. No man in worship, whether he leads it or shares in it, has any right to direct it according to his own personal preferences. He must seek the good of the whole worshipping fellowship. The great test of any part of worship is, "Will this help *everyone?*" It is not, "Will this display my special gifts?" It is, "Will this bring all here nearer to each other and nearer to God?"

(ii) *Worship must be intelligible.* The great things are essentially the simple things; the noblest language is essentially the simplest language. In the end only what satisfies my mind can comfort my heart, and only what my mind can grasp can bring strength to my life.

DAY TWENTY-EIGHT
The Words Reveal the Man
Romans 15:14–21

Brothers, I myself am quite sure that you, as you are, are full of goodness and replete with all knowledge and well able to give good advice to one another. I write to you with a certain amount of boldness, as it were, with the purpose of reminding you of what you already know. My ground for doing so is the God-given grace which made me the servant of Christ Jesus to the Gentiles, and gave me the sacred task of telling the good news, and my aim in doing so is to make the Gentiles an offering acceptable to God, an offering consecrated by the Holy Spirit. Now, in Christ, I have good reason to take a legitimate pride in my work in God's service. I can say this for I will not venture to speak of anything other than the things which Christ has wrought in me, by word and deed, by the power of signs and wonders, and by the power of the Holy Spirit, to bring the Gentiles into obedience to him. Thus from Jerusalem right round to Illyricum, I have completed the announcing of the good news of God's Anointed One. But it has always been my ambition to announce the good news, not where Christ's name has already been preached, because I want to avoid building on another man's foundation, but as it stands written: "Those to whom the good news has not been told shall see; and those who have not heard will understand."

Few passages reveal Paul's character better than this. He is coming to the end of his letter and is wishing to prepare the ground for the visit that he hopes soon to pay to Rome. Here we see something at least of his secret in winning men.

(i) Paul reveals himself as *a man of tact.* There is no rebuke here. He does not nag the brethren at Rome nor speak to them like some angry schoolmaster. He tells them that he is only reminding them of what they well know, and assures them that he is certain that they have it in them to render outstanding service to each other and to their Lord. Paul was much more interested in what a man could be than in what he was. He saw faults with utter clarity, and dealt with them with utter fidelity; but all the time he was thinking, not of the wretched creature that a man was, but of the splendid creature that he might be.

It is told that once when Michelangelo began to carve a huge and shapeless block of marble, he said that his aim was to release the angel imprisoned in the stone. Paul was like that. He did not want to knock a man down and out; he did not criticize to cause pain; he spoke with honesty and with severity but always because he wished to enable a man to be what he could be and never yet attained to being.

(ii) The only glory that Paul claimed was that he was *the servant of Christ.* The word he uses (*leitourgos*) is a great one. In ancient Greece there were certain state duties called *liturgies* (*leitourgiai*) which were sometimes laid upon and sometimes voluntarily shouldered by men who loved their country. There were five of these voluntary services which patriotic citizens used to undertake.

(*a*) There was *chorēgia,* which was the duty of supplying a chorus. When Aeschylus and Sophocles and Euripides were producing their immortal dramas, in each of them a verse-speaking chorus was necessary. There were great festivals like the City Dionysia when as many as eighteen new dramatic works were performed. Men who loved their city would volunteer to collect, maintain, instruct and equip such a chorus at their own expense.

(*b*) There was *gumnasiarchia.* The Athenians were divided into ten tribes; and they were great athletes. At certain of the great festivals there were the famous torch-races in which teams from the various tribes raced against each other. We still speak of *handing on the torch.* To win the torch-race was a great honour, and there were public-spirited men who at their own cost would select and support and train a team to represent their tribe.

(*c*) There was *hestiasis*. There were occasions when the tribes met together to share in a common meal and a common rejoicing; and there were generous men who undertook the task of meeting the expense of such a gathering.

(*d*) There was *archetheōria*. Sometimes the city of Athens sent an embassy to another city or to consult the oracle at Delphi or Dodona. On such an occasion everything had to be done in such a way that the honour of the city was maintained; and there were patriotic men who voluntarily defrayed the expenses of such an embassy.

(*e*) There was *triērarchia*. The Athenians were the great naval power of the ancient world. And one of the most patriotic things that a man could do was voluntarily to undertake the expenses of maintaining a trireme or warship for a whole year.

That is the background of this word *leitourgos*. In later days, as patriotism died, such liturgies became compulsory and not voluntary. Later the word came to be used of any kind of service; and later still it came to be used especially of worship and service rendered in the temple of the gods. But the word always had this background of generous service. Just as a man in the ancient days laid his fortune on the altar of the service of his beloved Athens, and counted it his only glory, so Paul laid his everything on the altar of the service of Christ, and was proud to be the servant of his Master.

(iii) Paul saw himself, in the scheme of things, as *an instrument in the hands of Christ*. He did not talk of what he had done; but of what Christ had done with him. He never said of anything: "I did it." He always said: "Christ used me to do it." It is told that the change in the life of D. L. Moody came when he went to a meeting and heard a preacher say: "If only one man would give himself entirely and without reserve to the Holy Spirit, what that Spirit might do with him!" Moody said to himself: "Why should I not be that man?" And all the world knows what the Spirit of God did with D. L. Moody. It is when a man ceases to think of what he can do and begins to think of what God can do with him, that things begin to happen.

(iv) Paul's ambition was to be a *pioneer*. It is told that when Livingstone volunteered as a missionary with the London Missionary

Society they asked him where he would like to go. "Anywhere," he said, "so long as it is forward." And when he reached Africa he was haunted by the smoke of a thousand villages which he saw in the distance. It was Paul's one ambition to carry the good news of God to men who had never heard it. He takes a text from *Isaiah* 52:15 to tell his aim:

> Ye armies of the living God,
> His sacramental host,
> Where hallowed footstep never trod,
> Take your appointed post.

DAY TWENTY-NINE

Lord and Christ

Acts 2:22–36

"Men of Israel, listen to these words. Jesus of Nazareth, a man approved by God to you by deeds of power and wonders and signs, which God, among you, did through him, as you yourselves know—this man, delivered up by the fore-ordained knowledge and counsel of God, you took and crucified by the hand of wicked men. But God raised him up and loosed the pains of death because it was impossible that he should be held subject by it. For David says in regard to him, 'Always I foresaw the Lord before me, because he is at my right hand so that I should not be shaken. Because of this my heart has rejoiced and my tongue has exulted, and, furthermore, my flesh shall dwell in hope, because thou wilt not leave my soul in the land of the dead nor wilt thou suffer thy Holy One to see corruption. Thou hast made known to me the ways of life. Thou shalt make me full of joy with thy countenance.' Brethren, I can speak to you freely about the patriarch David, that he is both dead and buried and his memorial is amongst us to this day. Thus he was a prophet; and because he knew that God had sworn an oath to him, that one of his descendants should sit upon his throne, he spoke with foresight about the resurrection of the Christ, that he would neither be left in the world of the dead nor would his flesh see corruption. This Jesus God raised up and all of us are his witnesses. So then when he had been exalted to the right hand of God

he received the promise of the Holy Spirit from the Father and poured out this which you see and hear. For David did not ascend up into heaven, and yet he says, 'The Lord said to my Lord, sit upon my right hand until I make thine enemies thy footstool for thy feet.' So then let all the house of Israel certainly know that God has made this Jesus whom you crucified Lord and Christ."

Here is a passage full of the essence of the thought of the early preachers.

(i) It insists that the Cross was no accident. It belonged to the eternal plan of God (verse 23). Over and over again *Acts* states this same thing (cf. 3:18; 4:28; 13:29). The thought of *Acts* safeguards us from two serious errors in our thinking about the death of Jesus. (*a*) The Cross is not a kind of emergency measure flung out by God when everything else had failed. It is part of God's very life. (*b*) We must never think that anything Jesus did changed the attitude of God to men. It was by God Jesus was sent. We may put it this way—the Cross was a window in time allowing us to see the suffering love which is eternally in the heart of God.

(ii) *Acts* insists that this in no way lessens the crime of those who crucified Jesus. Every mention of the crucifixion in *Acts* is instinct with a feeling of shuddering horror at the crime it was (cf. *Acts* 2:23; 3:13; 4:10; 5:30). Apart from anything else, the crucifixion shows supremely how horrifyingly sin can behave.

(iii) *Acts* is out to prove that the sufferings and death of Christ were the fulfillment of prophecy. The earliest preachers had to do that. To the Jew the idea of a crucified Messiah was incredible. Their law said, "A hanged man is accursed by God" (*Deuteronomy* 21:23). To the orthodox Jew the Cross made it completely impossible that Jesus could be the Messiah. The early preachers answered, "If you would only read your scriptures rightly you would see that all was foretold."

(iv) *Acts* stresses the resurrection as the final proof that Jesus was indeed God's Chosen One. *Acts* has been called The Gospel of the Resurrection. To the early Church the resurrection was all-important. We must remember this—*without the resurrection there would have been no Christian Church at all.* When the disciples preached the centrality of the resurrection they were arguing from experience. After the Cross they were bewildered, broken men, with their dream gone and their lives shattered. It was the resurrection which changed all that and turned them from cowards into heroes. It is one of the tragedies of the Church that so often the preaching of the resurrection is confined to Easter time. Every Sunday is the Lord's Day and every Lord's Day should be kept as resurrection day. In the Eastern Church on Easter day, when two people meet, one says, "The Lord is risen"; and the other answers, "He is risen indeed!" A Christian should never forget that he lives and walks with a Risen Lord.

DAY THIRTY

The Bliss of the Sufferer for Christ

Matthew 5:10–12

"Blessed are those who are persecuted for righteousness' sake, for theirs is the kingdom of heaven. Blessed are you when men revile you and persecute you and utter all kinds of evil against you falsely on my account. Rejoice and be glad for your reward is great in heaven, for so men persecuted the prophets who were before you."

One of the outstanding qualities of Jesus was his sheer honesty. He never left men in any doubt what would happen to them if they chose to follow him. He was clear that he had come "not to make life easy, but to make men great."

It is hard for us to realize what the first Christians had to suffer. Every department of their life was disrupted.

(i) Their Christianity might well disrupt their *work.* Suppose a man was a stone-mason. That seems a harmless enough occupation. But suppose his firm received a contract to build a temple to one of the heathen gods, what was that man to do? Suppose a man was a tailor, and suppose his firm was asked to produce robes for the heathen priests, what was that man to do? In a situation such as that in which the early Christians found themselves there was hardly any job in which a man might not find a conflict between his business interests and his loyalty to Jesus Christ.

The Church was in no doubt where a man's duty lay. More than a hundred years after this a man came to Tertullian with this very problem. He told of his business difficulties. He ended by saying, "What can I do? I must live!" "Must you?" said Tertullian. If it came to a choice between a loyalty and a living, the real Christian never hesitated to choose loyalty.

(ii) Their Christianity would certainly disrupt their *social* life. In the ancient world most feasts were held in the temple of some god. In very few sacrifices was the whole animal burned upon the altar. It might be that only a few hairs from the forehead of the beast were burned as a symbolic sacrifice. Part of the meat went to the priests as their perquisite; and part of the meat was returned to the worshipper. With his share he made a feast for his friends and his relations. One of the gods most commonly worshipped was Serapis. And when the invitations to the feast went out, they would read:

"I invite you to dine with me at the table of our Lord Serapis."

Could a Christian share in a feast held in the temple of a heathen god? Even an ordinary meal in an ordinary house began with a libation, a cup of wine, poured out in honor of the gods. It was like grace before meat. Could a Christian become a sharer in a heathen act of worship like that? Again the Christian answer was clear. The Christian must cut himself off from his fellows rather than by his presence give approval to such a thing. A man had to be prepared to be lonely in order to be a Christian.

(iii) Worst of all, their Christianity was liable to disrupt their *home* life. It happened again and again that one member of a family became a Christian while the others did not. A wife might become a Christian while her husband did not. A son or a daughter might become a Christian while the rest of the family did not. Immediately there was a split in the family. Often the door was shut forever in the face of the one who had accepted Christ.

Christianity often came to send, not peace, but a sword which divided families in two. It was literally true that a man might have to love Christ more than he loved father or mother, wife, or brother or sister. Christianity often involved in those days a choice between a man's nearest and dearest and Jesus Christ.

Still further, the penalties which a Christian had to suffer were terrible beyond description. All the world knows of the Christians who were flung to the lions or burned at the stake; but these were kindly deaths. Nero wrapped the Christians in pitch and set them alight, and used them as living torches to light his gardens. He sewed them in the skins of wild animals and set his hunting dogs upon them to tear them to death. They were tortured on the rack; they were scraped with pincers; molten lead was poured hissing upon them; red hot brass plates were affixed to the tenderest parts of their bodies; eyes were torn out; parts of their bodies were cut off and roasted before their eyes; their hands and feet were burned while cold water was poured over them to lengthen the agony. These things are not pleasant to think about, but these are the things a man had to be prepared for, if he took his stand with Christ.

We may well ask why the Romans persecuted the Christians. It seems an extraordinary thing that anyone living a Christian life should seem a fit victim for persecution and death. There were two reasons.

(i) There were certain slanders which were spread abroad about the Christians, slanders for which the Jews were in no small measure responsible. (*a*) The Christians were accused of cannibalism. The words of the Last Supper—"This is my body." "This cup is the New Testament in my blood"—were taken and twisted into a story that the Christians sacrificed a child and ate the flesh. (*b*) The Christians were accused of immoral practices, and their meetings were said to be orgies of lust. The Christian weekly meeting was called the *Agapē*, the Love Feast; and the name was grossly misinterpreted. Christians greeted each other with the kiss of peace; and the kiss of peace became a ground on which to build the slanderous accusations. (*c*) The Christians were accused of being incendiaries. It is true that they spoke of the coming end of the world, and they clothed their message in the apocalyptic pictures of the end of the world in flames. Their slanderers took these words and twisted them into threats of political and revolutionary incendiarism. (*d*) The Christians were accused of tampering with family relationships. Christianity did in fact split families as we have seen; and so Christianity was represented as something which divided man and wife, and disrupted the home. There were slanders enough waiting to be invented by malicious-minded men.

(ii) But the great ground of persecution was in fact political. Let us think of the situation. The Roman Empire included almost the whole known world, from Britain to the Euphrates, and from Germany to North Africa. How could that vast amalgam of peoples be somehow welded into one? Where could a unifying principle be found? At first it was found in the worship of the goddess Roma, the spirit of Rome. This was a worship which the provincial peoples were happy to give, for Rome had brought them peace and good government, and civil order and justice. The roads were cleared of brigands and the seas of pirates; the despots and tyrants had been banished by impartial Roman justice. The provincial was very willing to sacrifice to the spirit of the Empire which had done so much for him.

But this worship of Roma took a further step. There was one man who personified the Empire, one man in whom Roma might be felt to be incarnated, and that was the Emperor; and so the Emperor came to be regarded as a god, and divine honours came to be paid to him, and temples were raised to his divinity. The Roman government did not begin this worship; at first, in fact, it did all it could to discourage it. Claudius, the Emperor, said that he deprecated divine honors being paid to any human being. But as the years went on the Roman government saw in this Emperor-worship the one thing which could unify the vast Empire of Rome; here was the one center on which they all could come together. So, in the end, the worship of the Emperor became, not voluntary, but compulsory. Once a year a man had to go and burn a pinch of incense to the godhead of Caesar and say, "Caesar is Lord." And that is precisely what the Christians refused to do. For them Jesus Christ was the Lord, and to no man would they give that title which belonged to Christ.

It can be seen at once that Caesar-worship was far more a test of

political loyalty than anything else. In actual fact when a man had
burned his pinch of incense he received a certificate, a *libellus,* to say
that he had done so, and then he could go and worship any god he
liked, so long as his worship did not interfere with public order and
decency. The Christians refused to conform. Confronted with the
choice, "Caesar or Christ?" they uncompromisingly chose Christ.
They utterly refused to compromise. The result was that, however
good a man, however fine a citizen a Christian was, he was automatically an outlaw. In the vast Empire Rome could not afford pockets
of disloyalty, and that is exactly what every Christian congregation appeared to the Roman authorities to be. A poet has spoken of

The panting, huddled flock whose crime was Christ.

The only crime of the Christian was that he set Christ above Caesar; and for that supreme loyalty the Christians died in their thousands, and faced torture for the sake of the lonely supremacy of Jesus
Christ.

DAY THIRTY-ONE

Cooperation in Salvation

Philippians 2:12–18

*So then, my beloved, just as at all times you obeyed not only as in my pres-
ence, but much more, as things now are, in my absence, carry to its perfect conclusion the work of your own salvation with fear and trembling;
for it is God, who, that he may carry out his own good pleasure, brings to
effect in you both the initial willing and the effective action. Do all things
without murmurings and questionings, that you may show yourselves
blameless and pure, the spotless children of God in a warped and twisted
generation, in which you appear like lights in the world, as you hold forth
the word which is life, so that on the day of Christ it may be my proud
claim that I have not run for nothing and that I have not toiled for nothing. But if my own life is to be poured out on the sacrifice and service of
your faith, I rejoice and I do rejoice with you all. So also do you rejoice,
and share my rejoicing.*

Paul's appeal to the Philippians is more than an appeal to live in unity in a given situation; it is an appeal to live a life which will lead to the salvation of God in time and in eternity.

Nowhere in the New Testament is the work of salvation more succinctly stated. As the Revised Standard Version has it in verses 12 and 13: "Work out your own salvation with fear and trembling; for God's at work in you, both to will and to work for his good pleasure." As always with Paul, the words are meticulously chosen.

Work out your own salvation; the word he uses for work out is *katergazesthai,* which always has the idea of bringing to completion. It is as if Paul says: "Don't stop halfway; go on until the work of salvation is fully wrought out in you." No Christian should be satisfied with anything less than the total benefits of the gospel.

"For God is at *work* in you both to will and *to do* of his good pleasure." The word Paul uses for *work* and *do* is the same, the verb *energein.* There are two significant things about it; it is always used of *the action of God,* and it is always used of *effective action.* God's action cannot be frustrated, nor can it remain half-finished; it must be fully effective.

As we have said, this passage gives a perfect statement of the work of salvation.

(i) Salvation is of God. (*a*) It is God that works in us the desire to be saved. It is true that "our hearts are restless till they rest in him," and it is also true that "we could not even begin to seek him unless he had already found us." The desire for the salvation of God is not kindled by any human emotion but by God himself. The beginning of the process of salvation is awakened by God. (*b*) The continuance of that process is dependent on God. Without his help there can be no progress in goodness; without his help no sin can be conquered and no virtue achieved. (*c*) The end of the process of salvation is with God, for its end is friendship with God, in which we are his and he is ours. The work of salvation is begun, continued and ended in God.

(ii) There is another side to this. Salvation is of man. "Work out your own salvation," Paul demands. Without man's co-operation, even God is helpless. The fact is that any gift or any benefit has to be received. A man may be ill and the doctor able to prescribe the drugs that will cure him; but the man will not be cured until he takes them and he may stubbornly refuse all persuasion to take them. It is so with salvation. The offer of God is there; without it there can be no such thing as salvation. But no man can ever receive salvation unless he answers God's appeal and takes what he offers.

There can be no salvation without God, but what God offers man must take. It is never God who withholds salvation; it is always man who deprives himself of it.